Indian Vegetarian Cookery

JACK SANTA MARIA

Illustrated by Harry Baines

D1153869

RIDER AND COMPANY, LONDON

RIDER AND COMPANY
3 Fitzroy Square, London W1

AN IMPRINT OF THE HUTCHINSON GROUP

London Melbourne Sydney Auckland
Wellington Johannesburg Cape Town
and agencies throughout the world

First published 1973

*This book has been set in Spectrum type, printed in Great Britain
on cartridge paper by Anchor Press, and
bound by Wm. Brendon, both of Tiptree, Essex*
ISBN 0 09 116391 9 (paper)

OM. To the Mother of all cooks

'May the Ocean of Salt, the Ocean of Honey, the Ocean of Wine, the Ocean of Ghee, the Ocean of Curd, the Ocean of Milk, the Ocean of Sweet Water sprinkle thee with their consecrated waters.'

(From a consecration mantra—Mahānirvāna Tantra, X)

Contents

8

Acknowledgements

The author wishes to thank the Victoria and Albert Museum, London, for permission to use the nineteenth-century Indian painting for the cover illustration.

Special thanks are due to the following:
Mr Bhushan Puri, Uma and Jagdish, my first teachers.
Mrs Lucy Santa Maria, who inspired the creation of this book.
Mrs Eunice Santa Maria, for her recipes and constant help.
Sybil Santa Maria, for her recipes and help.
Mr Jacob Daniel, a connoisseur of Indian vegetarian cooking; and his wife Thelma, who is an excellent cook, for their recipes and help.
Mrs Bridget Fernandez, who finally procured grandmother's recipe!
Mr Biren Karmakar, who taught without trying.
Mrs Aladina, for her advice.
Daniel Brostoff, my editor, for his kind encouragement at all stages of publication.

Introduction

The seventeenth-century English traveller, Ovington, wrote in his *A Voyage to Surat* that 'Of all the regions of the Earth (India is) the only Public Theatre of Justice and Tenderness to Brutes and all living creatures.' He also found that, because of their diet, the Hindus kept a comely and proportionate body and lived a long life. The simple and meatless food made their thoughts 'quick and nimble', their 'comprehension of things' easier and developed in them a spirit of fearlessness.

With the increasing interest in Indian culture there has grown up in the West, at the same time, an interest in vegetarian food and today the vegetarian is no longer regarded as a crank. India, with her vast population of meat abstainers, has developed a rich and extensive range of vegetarian dishes. This book aims to present in simple terms a sample of this range especially for the vegetarian cook with the assurance that many of the recipes will tempt the meat and fish eater also. Cooking habits vary from area to area and recipes are included from all over the sub-continent to illustrate the variety of techniques and possibilities that are available to the vegetarian cook.

In former times, India was a land rich in the variety and quantity of its foodstuffs. Foreign visitors to India, from the beginning of the seventeenth century onwards, have noted with amazement the abundance and cheapness of an enormous number of foods and food products in the bazaars and markets of towns and cities all over the country. Poets of the Mughal era (1556–1784), such as Sur Das, describe the typical fare of the time. Morning breakfast (*kalevā*) consisted of a variety of fruits and sweets, besides bread and butter, milk or curd. Bread was made of mixed wheat and gram flour. Also served at breakfast were pakoris, jalebis, laddus, malpuras, chironjis, raisins, almonds, pistachio nuts, coconuts, bananas, mangoes, apricots, cashew nuts, water melons and dry dates. Luncheon included kachoris (stuffed puris), luchchis (special fried bread), khichhari, milk, butter, ghee, honey, dry fruits, vegetables, papads, lemons, ginger, pickles, various pulses and grams. Out of such a rich and nutritious diet the basic dishes of Indian cooking had, by this time, already crystallised.

Both climate and environment have influenced cooking and eating habits, producing distinct regional variations. These variations are reflected in the cuisine of the four major cities of Delhi, Madras, Bombay and Calcutta. In the North, where wheat is grown, breads rather than rice form the staple part of the diet. The influence of Middle-Eastern neighbours can be seen in 'Mughlai' cooking techniques such as pulau rice and tanduri baking. The tandur is a barrel-shaped mud or clay oven made out of doors. As well as bread, this oven is used for other special tanduri dishes. Rice or khichhari usually accompanies curries, one of the most popular of which is made from peas and potatoes. Vegetables are prepared as bhujias or bhartas. Dals are eaten at nearly every meal in a variety of forms. Curd (yogurt) is a nourishing addition along with pickles and chutneys. Desserts and sweetmeats made from milk may follow, especially firni and varieties of khir and halva.

South India is noted for its vegetarian and rice dishes which are hotter though not as rich as in the North. Coconut products feature prominently in the cooking and many typically Northern dishes may be found, changed only by the addition of some coconut. Towards the end of the meal the rice may be mixed with yogurt, which has a cooling effect. Pachadi, seasoned yogurt, like the Northern raita, may also be served. South Indian breakfasts include idlis, steamed rice cakes, and dosas, pancakes made with various flours, accompanied by chutneys or sambhar, a hot lentil soup. South Indian coffee, which is among the world's best in quality, is drunk with milk and sugar and served at any time of the day.

In Western India, vegetarian food takes on a Gujerati or Maharashtri character. Here a sweet is served at the beginning of the meal and is eaten with a puri or chapati, followed by vegetable dishes and curried lentils. Some Western cooks like to sweeten lentils and vegetable preparations. The meal usually ends with rice though less rice tends to be eaten in the West than in the South or East. Popular desserts are milk sweets made from rice and nuts and shrikand, yogurt sweetened and seasoned with cardamon and saffron. In Maharashtra it is common to eat a vegetable dish and puris with shrikand. Bhel puri is a notable savoury snack sold all over Bombay and made a speciality by certain restaurants.

In Bengal, where rice and dals are popular, many vegetarians eat fish. This sometimes poses problems for Hindus from the South who go visiting in the East! Bengali or East Indian food is plainer, with rice forming the main part along with luchchis, a fried bread like a puri. Desserts are more simple, ranging from milk-sweetened yogurt (*mishti dhoi*) to various milk sweets like sandesh, rasmalai and gulab jamun. Bengal is famous for its sweets and the fat cheeks of children are often compared to the favourite Bengali delicacy, rasgullas.

According to the Yogis of old, food, like other matter, may be classified as possessing three distinct qualities, or a mixture of these. These are *tamas*, the quality of inertia and dullness; *rajas*, the quality of action and the excitement of the mind and body; and *sattva*, the quality of harmony and the elevation of the spirit. Certain foodstuffs can be quickly classified under one of these headings. Chilli, for example, is an obvious rajasic ingredient. Some ancient authorities go further and classify the root vegetables as tamasic in tendency since they grow underground, in the darkness. Those foods which grow and develop in the air, above ground level, are considered more sattvic.

The Mahabharata, in a verse of the Shānti Parva, refers to the necessity of ensuring purity in food and drink as one of the ten essential disciplines of life (273.15). The Bhagavad Gītā distinguishes temperament according to the kind of food we prefer. Those foods liked by the sattvic personality are savoury and oleaginous, substantial and agreeable, and they increase life, energy, strength, health, joy and cheerfulness. Foods liked by the rajasic are excessively bitter, sour, salty, pungent, or dry and burning. They will cause pain, grief and disease, says the Gīta. Tamasic people prefer food which is stale, tasteless, rotten or left over. These qualities refer to food that has lost its nutritious value due to bad cooking, faulty preparation or putrefaction (XVII. 8–10).

The meal as a whole should therefore be planned as a harmonious, sattvic, one. If spice or acid is used, balance it with something bland. The meal that leaves one heavy and full of sleep has also filled one with the quality of tamas. An overspiced meal that overstimulates the digestive organs or excites the nervous system is rajasic. After a sattvic meal we should feel contented without feeling full. 'Eat till your stomach is three-quarters full and leave one quarter for the Lord.' This wise saying allows one to fully appreciate the food as well as giving the digestive system a chance to operate efficiently.

In India, those who follow the Hindu code of *ahimsa* (non-injury) believe this to mean that the avoidance of injury to living beings is a virtue worthy to be practised at all times, even when one feels hungry! This has in no way inhibited the Indian's ingenuity and zest for life which is expressed so dramatically in the art of cooking. Food and eating are divine gifts and the whole affair, from preparation to consumption, should be carried out in a reverential and joyful manner. Each stage in the preparation is an art which the true cook is loath to give up to the machinations of some new gadget. However, the Western cook, unlike the peaceful villager, does not have the time to stir some sweet dish for several gentle hours, or to roast and grind the spices daily so that they are always fresh for the curry. As far as possible, these more lengthy processes have been eliminated in the recipes and the 'short-cuts' which the average Indian housewife of the city herself uses have been suggested.

Traditionally, Indian cooking has been handed down by demonstration and word of mouth from mother to daughter, or father to son and, as in most other countries, the excellent male cook is a priceless treasure acknowledged by all levels of society. The master chef of the ancient courts was esteemed like the master musician, astrologer or painter and was indeed an artist in his own right. The great chefs specialised in certain areas of cooking and separately explored the arts of rice, vegetables, sweetmeats, and so on, till the magical potions of today were realised.

By the use of subtle aromatic spices and the natural aroma of steamed and fried vegetables, fruits and nuts, the diner is first tempted to eat. Then the eyes are alternately delighted by a range of colour and texture, from the soothing whites of delicate raitas and rice dishes to the glowing reds of sauces and pickles. It is in the range and variety of Indian cooking that the full potential of vegetable food is realised. By developing your experience of Indian cuisine, boldness, style and adventure become the keynote of your vegetable cooking. Delight and wonder pervade the kitchen and your meat-eating friends will only admire your ingenuity and panache.

Having married into a family of excellent cooks, I am also fortunate in having friends and relations from all parts of India who have provided me with much valuable information as well as being the best of culinary critics. I thank them for their help, especially my wife who had the final word in passing all the recipes. I hope that, having mastered these, you will feel stimulated to pursue your own investigations further.

The Cook's Story

India is a land of stories and story-tellers. Very often the cook is
one such story-teller, having plenty of time in which to invent
stories and in which to perfect them. When cooks meet their friends
they not only discuss the culinary arts but may frequently while
away the time exchanging stories, many of which start life as an
actual occurrence. In the house of a certain learned pandit, the
celebrated cook Deviprasad was entertaining an old friend from
Bangalore. After rinsing their mouths with scented water, the
two friends settled down to a smoke and to talk about old times.
'You know,' said the cook's friend, 'these merchants are great
yarners. You never know whether to believe anything they tell
you.' 'That's true,' agreed the cook. 'And you never know whether
they're really trying to sell you something.' 'Well, I met quite an
agreeable one on my way here as a matter of fact. He told me an
odd story which only made me realise what a cunning old devil
he was.' 'Go on!' urged the cook, 'what did he have to say then?'
The friend took a puff at his smoke while they both eased
themselves into a more comfortable position . . .

Utensils and Serving

From the Indian point of view, since eating is a divine necessity, food must possess this divine nature and the cook acts accordingly. First, he prepares himself for the task in hand. He bathes and purifies himself after ensuring that the kitchen and utensils to be used are clean. Then, all the ingredients are carefully washed, where this may be necessary, and prepared. Tasting the food during the cooking process is usually avoided and the cook comes to know by experience the correct proportions that suit the tastes of the family.

A satisfactory and balanced meal might consist of two or three vegetable dishes, one of which is lentils, rice, some pickles or chutney, yogurt, and a sweet dish. This may be filled out on special occasions by the addition of more vegetable dishes, a greater ranger of chutneys, and a salad. Finally, nuts and dried or fresh fruit may be passed round with some little dishes of digestives such as fennel seed (*sānf*), cardamon (*elaichi*) and a sweet *pān* mixture. Any one of the range of Indian breads (*rotīs*) may accompany or be substituted for the rice and as these are often made unleavened from wholemeal flour (*ātā*) they will provide a nourishing change from your rice cookery. Pappadams, thin crispy biscuits made from gram flour, may be served with rice or rotis.

Traditionally, food is served on a polished circular metal tray (a large one is termed a *thal* and the smaller individual one a *thali*) which contains the different dishes and chutneys in separate metal or earthenware bowls. These individual bowls are known as *katorīs*. Rice or bread is kept in the middle of the tray and the diner helps himself to the food in any order he wishes. Lacking these items, the Western cook could easily substitute a set of ordinary china bowls or dishes and a serving plate for each person. Disposable plates were invented long ago in the form of banana leaves and in South India these large leaves are still used for this purpose.

Use heavy pans wherever possible, a deep frying pan is always useful. Since stainless steel covers all uses, this is to be preferred. Keep a separate non-stick pan for sweet things only. A concave iron dish (*tava*) for chapati-making can be purchased at many Asian stores. Wooden spoons are preferable to metal ones; those used for rice, sweet cooking and spicy dishes being kept for each of these uses only. Separate chopping boards should be kept for vegetables and spices, and for nuts and sweet ingredients. A range of metal sieves and a colander will come in handy at all times. A pestle and mortar is a necessity but care should be taken to ensure that no acids or strong alkalis come in contact with a metal one. A good grinder may be used for these purposes but cannot be substituted for the pounding function of the pestle and mortar. Blenders and liquidisers are useful tools but the use of the pressure cooker, which cooks by a different process to steaming or '*damming*', produces a result that is entirely opposed to the desired aim, namely, the retention of vital food elements.

The Spices

CARDAMON (*elaichi*): this member of the ginger family (*Elettaria cardamomum*) is a pungent aromatic, often chewed after eating as a digestive and breath-sweetener, and a primary ingredient in *garam masāla*. It may be used whole in pods or the seeds removed and crushed or ground. The white pods are generally used in sweet things and the green in other preparations.

CHILLI (*mirch*): The seed pods of *Capsicum annum*. When fresh they are green or red. The dried red pods are used whole or ground to make chilli powder. Chillies impart a distinct flavour to a dish as well as making it very hot. The powder also gives a red colour to a dish. If chillies are excluded, the red colour may still be retained by adding paprika powder in its place. Paprika is a close relative of the hot chilli, having a distinct flavour like other capsicums, but it does not make the dish hot.

CINNAMON (*dalchini*): The dried inner bark of cassia (*Cinnamomum cassia*) is another ingredient in curries and sweet dishes alike. Being an aromatic, it may be chewed to sweeten the breath and is said to strengthen the gums. True cinnamon (*Cinnamomum zeylanicum*) has a more delicate flavour than cassia and is not as pungent. This makes it more suitable for sweet dishes.

CLOVES (*laūng*): The dried fruit of *Myrtus caryophyllus* has always been the basis of the spice trade. Clove oil is antiseptic and strongly aromatic and an essential ingredient in *garam masāla*.

CORIANDER (*dhania*): *Coriandrum sativum* is an annual plant in the Umbelliferous family like Cow Parsley. Its fresh leaves are used in the same way as parsley is used in the West, indeed, parsley may be substituted for the fresh leaves when these are not available, though the flavour will not be the same. Now one of the most commonly used herbs in the world, coriander leaves were used in England up to the time of Elizabeth I. The seeds are highly aromatic and are used ground or whole in curries, pulaus and other savoury dishes.

CUMIN (*jīra*): The seeds of black cumin, *Cuminum nigrum* (*kāla jīra*) and white cumin, *Cuminum cyminum* (*safed jīra*) are also used whole or ground in sweet or savoury dishes. The whole seeds are an essential ingredient in certain pulaus. Cumin, like coriander, is a member of the parsley family.

CURRY LEAVES (*kari patta*): The pungent aromatic leaves of *Chalcas koenigii* taste like *garam masāla*. Thrown in whole or broken, they give a characteristic flavour to many South Indian dishes. In Tamil the leaves are referred to as *karuvepila* and in Hindi as *katnīm* or *mītha nīm*. They may be dried if purchased fresh and stored in an airtight jar till needed.

FENNEL (*sānf*): The small, elongated, pale green seeds of *Foenculum vulgare* taste like aniseed or liquorice. They are one of the seeds handed round after a meal both as a digestive and as a breath-sweetener, though they are sometimes used in curries.

FENUGREEK (*methi*): The leaves of this plant, *Trigonella fenumgraecum*, have a strong flavour and aroma. Less dried methi should be used than fresh. The lightly roasted seeds are used in curries and influence the texture of a dish.

GINGER (*adrak*): The dried spicy rhizomes of *Zingiber officinalis* are used extensively in all forms of cooking. The fresh root is usually preferred to the powder. It is considered an aid to digestion and induces sweating.

GUR is unrefined Indian cane sugar with a crude but individual taste and quality.

MINT (*podina*): The fresh leaves are used in a way similar to that of Western cooking, often as a garnish. It is also an ingredient in chutneys.

MUSTARD SEED (*rai*): A tiny round dark brown seed (*Brassica juncea*) which is highly nutritious. Care has to be taken when frying as the seeds tend to jump from the pan. The leaf of field mustard, *sarson*

(*Brassica campestris*) is cooked like spinach. Mustard oil is used in cooking particularly in Bengal and North India.

POPPY SEED (*khus khus*): 900,000 of these tiny seeds are said to make up a pound ($\frac{1}{2}$ kilo). Their colour ranges from creamy white to grey and black. They stimulate the appetite and tend to thicken sauces. Only seeds of the opium poppy (*Papaver somniferum*) are used.

SAFFRON (*kesha*): This is perhaps the most expensive of all spices. It is the dried stigmata of the saffron crocus, *Crocus sativus*, which have to be harvested by hand. It can colour many thousands of times its own weight of water and is usually soaked in warm water or milk to extract the brilliant yellow colour. Turmeric should not be used as a substitute.

SESAME SEED (*til*): Tiny white, highly nutritious seeds giving a particularly nutty flavour. Sesame oil is a sweet oil used for cooking in some parts of the country.

SUGAR: Two unrefined Indian sugar products may be found in Indian and Oriental grocers. They are excellent substitutes for brown sugar and it worth buying a little to experience their special individual flavours and quality. *Jaggery* is unrefined palm sugar. It is delicious with fresh coconut as a sweet. *Gur* is unrefined cane sugar with a crude but enjoyable flavour.

TAMARIND (*imali*): The seed pod and attached plant material of *Tamarindus indica* which is soaked in warm water to extract its acidic watery pulp. In most cases it is preferable to vinegar where tartness or piquancy is required.

TURMERIC (*haldi*): The dried fleshy root of another member of the ginger family (*Circuma longa*). It contains a bright yellow pigment and the saffron robes of holy men are often dyed with it. To be used for this purpose, it must be made fast or the colour will run. It is a principal ingredient in curries, but, like chilli, is one to be respected. The warm and pungent flavour is very strong and too much turmeric will overwhelm and ruin a dish. It is often used to colour rice when thrown into the boiling water after the rice.

Essential Spice Recipes

If you are intending to develop your knowledge of Indian vegetable cooking, you should avoid the use of 'curry powders' and get used to making your own powders and pastes or *masālas* as they are known. Like all the other techniques, this is part of the craft. The Tamil word *kari* means a sauce or stew. A curry is prepared by stewing the food with a masala, a mixture of spices. This may either be served with the sauce or cooked until dry. The advantage in developing your own range of masalas is that you will quickly obtain the exact taste which your dishes require and leave the stamp of individuality upon them. Masalas are designed to suit the particular ingredients and techniques indicated in the recipes. As the recipes show, various forms of specific spices are mixed in special ways to produce the result. The substitution of a blanket curry powder or paste for these special mixtures will obviously produce a completely different result. Like curry powder, the masalas listed below may be purchased already made up but these cannot match the fragrance and freshness of the homemade product.

It is worthwhile grinding the spices together from the whole seed when making up a masala. Sometimes this may involve grinding them with garlic, ginger or some other plant. Compare the result with using the pre-powdered ingredients. You may feel that it is more satisfying to take a little time and trouble to get the subtlety and freshness that home-grinding gives to your dish. If a recipe suggests this procedure, you can alternatively use powders and chop the other spices if speed and convenience are required.

GARAM MASĀLA is a condiment added to a dish at a late stage in the cooking, often just before serving. Sometimes it is used as a flavouring agent in cold dishes such as *raitas*. A simple garam masala may be made by grinding $\frac{1}{2}$ cup of green cardamon seeds, 1 cup cumin seeds

27

and ⅛ cup of cloves. Mix together and store in an airtight jar. Two more garam masala recipes are given below:

1. Grind together 3 parts cardamom seeds, 3 parts cinnamon, 1 part cloves, 1 part cumin seed.
2. Grind together 4 parts black peppercorns, 4 parts coriander seed, 3 parts cumin seed or fennel seed, 1 part cloves, 1 part cardamom seed, 1 part cinnamon.

Bay leaf, nutmeg and mace feature in the recipes of some cooks. As may be seen from the above ingredients and their proportions, the final taste and aroma of the masala is a matter of personal choice and any number of variations can be made up from some 16 different spices.

Kashmir has developed its own cooking style which has been influenced by Mughal culture. A simple recipe for Kashmiri garam masala is given here and should be used where the recipe calls for this particular masala:

Grind together 4 parts cardamom seed, 3 parts cumin seed, 1 part black peppercorns, 1 part cinnamon, 1 part cloves. Add a pinch of mace and nutmeg and store. Sometimes chilli and salt are added to this recipe with a few drops of water. The masala then approaches the consistency of a paste and may be taken as it is and used as a condiment like a pickle or chutney.

In South India a particular masala is used known as *sambhar* or Madras Rasam. Fry the ingredients separately before grinding and mixing: 4 parts split black beans (*dāl urhad*), 4 parts coriander seeds, 4 parts cumin seed, 2 parts black peppercorns, 1 part fenugreek seeds. A hotter sambhar, imparting a quite different flavour, can be made by grinding and mixing 1 part crushed curry leaves with 1 part mustard seed, 1 part fenugreek seed, 1 part cumin seed, 6 parts coriander seed, 6 parts dry red chillies and 1 part black peppercorns.

Basic Ingredients

GHĪ: Ghee is clarified butter or margarine in which the water and any impurities have been driven off by heating. Good quality ghee is available in tins and vegetable ghee is also of excellent quality. If you want to make your own, place either butter or margarine in a saucepan and simmer for about an hour. Strain and store in a glass jar or clean tin. Ghee is the traditional cooking medium of India from Vedic times when it was known in Sanskrit as *ghrit*. Mustard oil and sweet (sesame) oil are the main cooking oils in use in certain regions of the country and each imparts its own particular flavour to the dish. Safflower, peanut or any other vegetable oil may be substituted where ghee is indicated in the recipes. When very hot, ghee becomes still, oil starts to bubble.

DAHI: Curd or yogurt is homemade by the country people. The dahi-seller deals in this commodity alone and makes it in enormous bowls. Plain, commercial yogurt is a handy substitute. Dahi can be made by mixing a tablespoon of cultured yogurt with a pint ($\frac{1}{2}$ litre) of boiled lukewarm milk. Keep the mixture in a warm place or incubator for about 4 hours at above body temperature (43°C). When it has set the curd is ready. Keep some back to make the next lot of dahi. True yogurt is formed by the action of a number of special bacteria and fungi so commercial yogurt made of skimmed milk and milk solids, chemically soured, will not do. A simple incubator can be made by fitting a small box with an electric bulb and a place to store a bowl of curd. Once a routine is established, real yogurt can be enjoyed in the home every day.
Curd is used in India as an ingredient in cooking and is also eaten as it is along with the food. It is readily digested and is a nourishing accompaniment to any meal. Its slightly tart flavour makes a pleasing change or substitute for a more acid pickle or chutney. A certain nursery rhyme seems to indicate that curd was once also relished in

England. Perhaps the practitioners of Indian vegetarian cookery will help to make this healthy food popular once more.

CHENNA: Indian cottage cheese is made by putting dahi in a muslin bag and allowing it to drip overnight until the excess water is removed. If this cheese is pressed with a heavy weight till it hardens, the result is known as *panir*. Panir is cooked in cubes with vegetables and is, like chenna, an ingredient in certain sweetmeats. Ordinary cheese cannot be substituted for panir since it liquefies when heated.

KHOYA: If fresh milk is boiled in a heavy pan for an hour or so, stirring to prevent sticking, a thick residue results. This khoya is the basis of many sweetmeats, though the cooking process is laborious. Khoya may be made from full-cream powdered milk by working 1½ tablespoons of hot water into every 2 ounces (60 g) of powder to make 3 ounces (85 g) of khoya.

FLOURS, ĀTĀ, BESAN AND RICE FLOUR: Ata is a wholegrain flour which can only be bought in Asian grocers or healthfood stores since it is not the wholemeal flour sold by English bakers. When mixed with water it often takes on a distinctly sticky consistency.

When gram is ground the flour is known as *besan*. Many other members of the pea and bean family are made into a flour in India for use in pastry, batters, pancakes and as ingredients in certain dishes. These flours should be popular with vegetarians and healthfood enthusiasts since they contain the whole grain and have nothing added to them.

Rice flour is used both in sweets such as *phirni* where it functions like cornflour in Western dishes of a similar nature, and in pancakes and chapatis. A nourishing pancake (*dosa*) is made for breakfast in South India in which rice flour and urhad dal flour are used.

COCONUT PRODUCTS: Coconut is used in Western and Southern style cooking. Make two holes in the natural depressions at the top of the coconut. Pour off the water. Tap round the middle of the shell with a hammer till it breaks in half. The white flesh can now be grated or chopped.

Coconut milk is made by extracting the juice from the white flesh.

The process can be speeded up by adding a little hot water to the coconut flakes. It is always preferable to use fresh coconut, but creamed coconut is a great time saver. You can buy this as a block which is cut up and hot water is then added to make the coconut milk.

In Britain, if any difficulty is experienced in procuring ingredients, these London stockists will supply by post:
The Bombay Emporium Ltd, Radiant House, Pegamoid Road,
  London N18
Messrs Patak Ltd, Drummond Street, NW1.

Weights and Measures

Simple weights and measures are provided as a starting point for your own experimentation. These may be varied according to taste. The Indian housewife is used to guessing the amounts of various ingredients and she only uses more accurate measuring when preparing larger quantities of food. Even then she will tend to judge by hand and sight according to the amount of raw materials available. In one family, two cooks using the same ingredients and same quantities will still produce different results and this is all part of the fascination. Try combinations of dishes that suit your taste but always aim at a light and balanced meal.

Here is a comparison between Imperial and Metric systems:
  approximately ½ litre (500 ml) = approximately 18 fluid oz
  approximately 30 grams   = approximately 1 oz
  approximately 450 grams   = approximately 1 lb

The cup measurement in this book is one which holds 8 fluid ounces (250 ml) of water, 8 oz (225 g) of sugar, 5 oz (140 g) of flour, 6 oz (170 g) of rice.

A teaspoon holds approximately ⅙ fluid ounce (5 ml), a dessertspoon approximately ½ fluid ounce (14 ml) and a tablespoon approximately 1 fluid ounce (28 ml), an ounce (28 g) of ghee or an ounce of sugar.

All measures given in this book are level ones. Though spoon and cup sizes vary, the intelligent cook will soon find out the amounts needed to obtain the desired results.

The recipes are sufficient for 4–6 people.

The Tale of the Merchant

'Well,' his friend began, 'apparently it was rumoured that smuggling was going on, though who it was or what was being smuggled was not entirely known. One of the suspects, a rice merchant, was always stopped on his way into the town by the guards appointed to the task. Each time the guards asked the merchant to empty his rice sacks so that they could be thoroughly searched and each time they found nothing. So the merchant was allowed to go on his way into the town. Once they soaked his sacks in water, along with all his clothes. Another time the entire contents were burnt but nothing was ever found. Some years later, the merchant happened to bump into one of the guards in the copper bazaar and they fell into conversation. "Do you remember all that smuggling during the time of the famine?" asked the merchant. "Oh, yes, I remember," smiled the guard. "Tell me, did they ever catch the fellow?" "No," replied the guard, "they never caught him. Why, did you hear who it was?" "It was me," said the merchant. "You" How could it be you? We searched you and never found anything. How could you be the smuggler?" "I was smuggling rice," replied the merchant . . .'

Rice

The staple food of millions of Asians has, like wheat, many varieties. Twenty-six kinds of rice are noted in the *Padmavat* of Malik Mohammad Jayasi in 1540. The most popular strains used in savoury cooking are the long-grained ones of which the Patna type are best known. Basmatti rice is probably the best which can be bought in England. Whatever the technique to be used in cooking, always soak and wash the rice beforehand in at least three waters.

Plain boiled rice is the main item of food in South India and Bengal and Assam in the North-East. Pulau, brought by the Persians and desert men of the West, has since become popular all over the country. The tantalisingly elusive fragrance and flavour of a well-prepared pulau is an international language known throughout the Middle East.

Grains of rice, symbolising prosperity, wealth and fertility, are sprinkled during *pūjās* (acts of worship). Diagrams drawn during various religious rites are frequently made in coloured rice powders, and decoration in this medium has become an art form in its own

34

right. It is considered auspicious to fill the bowl of a wandering holy man (*sādhu*) with some cooked rice and the Hindu priest is sometimes presented with a bag of rice after conducting a religious ceremony.

Plain Rice (*Chāval*)

There are many ways of preparing plain boiled rice but they all benefit from the rice having been soaked in water before cooking. Soaking time may vary from five minutes to a few hours. Always wash the rice thoroughly before leaving it to soak.

The simplest technique is to empty 1½ cups of washed and drained rice into a saucepan of boiling water with 1–2 teaspoonfuls of salt. In 10–12 minutes the rice should be ready, the grains tender but firm. Pour into a metal colander and leave to drain. The grains should be separate from each other, not mushy and stuck together.

Variety with Plain Rice

In parts of the North West Frontier Region, the boiled rice is drained and returned to the pan with 2 tablespoons of ghee or butter and a teaspoon of cumin seeds or powder. This makes the rice a little rich and spicy. Stirring in some cooked vegetables at the end can, in the same way, make your plain rice more interesting.

Plain boiled rice can be made both rich and colourful by adding nuts, sultanas and five spices (*pānch pūran*), and colouring the grains with turmeric. Fry half a cup of finely chopped onion, cashew nuts and sultanas separately. In South India, grated coconut would be added along with the nuts and sultanas. Stir into the cooked and drained rice. Fry half a teaspoon each of fennel seeds, cumin seeds, fenugreek seeds, poppy seeds and mustard seeds with a teaspoon of turmeric in 2 tablespoons of ghee. Stir into the rice and mix well till all the rice has become yellow. Other seeds such as sesame and caraway go equally well in such a mixture which may be varied according to taste.

In Maharashtra, plain rice is sometimes cooked by boiling it in diluted coconut milk, using 1 coconut to a pound (½ kilo) of rice. Colour the milk with ½ teaspoon of turmeric powder. When the rice is nearly cooked, keep the heat low and throw in a finely chopped onion, fried, salt, 6 cloves and 10 peppercorns.

Some cooks like all the water to be absorbed in the cooking, as in pulau rice. For this the water has to be judged correctly. 1 cup of Basmatti rice absorbs about 2 cups of water.

Plain Pulau Rice

Indian pulau, apart from being very like its Middle-Eastern ancestors, has relations in Spain and Italy also—the paella and risotto.

The simplest savoury rice is made by frying 1½ cups of washed and drained rice in a tablespoon of ghee for a few minutes. First the grains become translucent then white and opaque. Add 3 cups of boiling water and 1½ teaspoons of salt. Bring to the boil, cover and simmer gently till all the liquid is absorbed. This last part of the process may be finished off in a moderate oven. The grains should be tender and separate. A tastier plain pulau can be made using the following ingredients:

1½ cups rice
2 tablespoons ghee
1 onion, sliced
4 cloves garlic, finely chopped
1 inch piece (2·5 cm) ginger, finely chopped
6 cloves
2 inches (5 cm) cinnamon, broken

½ teaspoon paprika or chilli powder
2 green cardamoms
1 teaspoon garam masala
1 teaspoon cumin seeds
1½ teaspoons salt
3 cups water or vegetable stock, boiling
chopped fresh coriander leaves for garnish

Fry half the onion with the garlic in ghee till golden. Add the rest of the ingredients and the drained rice and stir fry till the grains become opaque. Add the boiling water or stock, bring to the boil, cover and simmer gently till all the liquid is absorbed and the rice is cooked. Meanwhile fry the rest of the onion to garnish with the chopped coriander leaf.

Peas Pulau (*Matar pulau*)

This can be made in the same way. Add 1½ cups of fresh peas at the beginning of the frying, or if frozen, at the end: this prevents them becoming too soft. Fry a sliced onion and 10 almonds and use to garnish with a sliced hard-boiled egg (optional), tomatoes, cucumber and chopped coriander leaves. Serve with a vegetable curry and beaten yogurt.

Mushroom Pulau (*Khumbi pulau*)

1½ cups rice
1 onion, sliced
2 tablespoons ghee
6 oz (170 g) mushrooms, sliced
4 oz (113 g) panir (optional)

1½ teaspoons salt
4 oz (113 g) peas
1 green chilli, chopped
    (optional)
3 cups water or vegetable stock

Fry the onion in ghee till golden. Stir in the drained rice, mushrooms, panir and salt. Fry for 5 minutes. Add peas and chilli, hot water or stock, cover and simmer till cooked. Stir in frozen peas at the end of the cooking.

Cauliflower Pulau (*Phūlgobi pulau*)

1½ cups rice
2 tablespoons ghee
8 oz (225 g) cauliflower sprigs
1 onion, chopped
6 cloves garlic, finely chopped
2 green cardamoms
2 inches (5 cm) cinnamon,
    broken
6 cloves

1 inch (2·5 cm) piece ginger,
    finely chopped
2 green chillies, chopped
    (optional)
½ teaspoon paprika or chilli
    powder
2 teaspoons salt
1 teaspoon cumin seeds
½ teaspoon garam masala
1 cup yogurt

Wash, soak and drain the rice. Sprinkle the cauliflower sprigs with salt and pepper and fry in ghee till they begin to turn golden. Remove from the ghee and fry the onion and garlic. Add cardamoms, cinnamon, cloves and the drained rice. Stir-fry till the rice turns opaque.

Add the cauliflower, ginger, chillies, paprika, salt, cumin seeds and garam masala. Fry for a further 5 minutes. Stir in the yogurt. Add 3 cups of hot water, bring to the boil, cover and simmer till cooked. Garnish according to taste.

Vegetable Pulau (*Sabzī pulau*)

1½ cups rice
1 inch (2·5 cm) piece ginger
2 green chillies, chopped
  (optional)
a few bay leaves, broken
1 tablespoon chopped
  coriander leaf
½ teaspoon turmeric powder

3 tablespoons ghee
1 onion, finely chopped
1 teaspoon garam masala
8 oz (225 g) peas
8 oz (225 g) green beans,
  chopped
8 oz (225 g) tomatoes, quartered
1½ teaspoons salt

Wash the rice, soak and leave to drain. Grind the ginger, chillies, bay leaf and coriander with the turmeric powder. Heat ghee and lightly fry the onions with the garam masala. Add the ginger paste and rice and fry till the rice is opaque. Add the vegetables and salt and fry for a further few minutes. Pour in 3 cups of hot water and bring to the boil. Cover and simmer gently till the rice is cooked.

Vegetable and Lentil Pulau (*Sabzī dāl pulau*)

1 cup mixed lentils
1 tablespoon coriander seeds
2¼ teaspoons salt
1½ cups rice
5 tablespoons ghee
1 onion, chopped
4 cloves garlic, finely chopped
6 cloves
4 green cardamoms
2 inches (5 cm) cinnamon,
  broken
1 lb (450 g) mixed vegetables,
  chopped

1 inch (2·5 cm) piece ginger,
  finely chopped
2 green chillies, chopped
  (optional)
1 teaspoon ground black
  pepper
2 bay leaves, broken
3 tomatoes, quartered
4 oz (113 g) spinach or greens
4 oz (113 g) panir cubes, fried
  till golden
chopped coriander leaf

Wash and soak the lentils for an hour. Drain and cook in water with coriander seeds and a teaspoon of salt till tender but not mushy. Strain and keep the liquid.

Meanwhile, soak and drain the rice. Heat 2 tablespoons ghee and lightly fry the onion and garlic. Add rice, cloves, cardamoms, cinnamon and fry till the rice turns opaque. Make up the lentil water to 3 cups with hot water and add to the rice with $1\frac{1}{2}$ teaspoons of salt. Bring to the boil, cover and simmer gently. While the rice is cooking, fry the chopped vegetables till tender in 2 tablespoons ghee, with the ginger, chillies, pepper, bay leaves and tomatoes.

Fry the drained lentils with chopped spinach in a tablespoon of ghee for a few minutes. Five minutes before the rice is cooked, stir in the lentils, vegetables and fried panir. Serve garnished with chopped coriander leaf.

Yellow Rice Pulau

$1\frac{1}{2}$ cups rice
2 tablespoons ghee
2 onions, sliced
a few curry leaves
10 peppercorns
4 cloves
1 teaspoon turmeric powder

3 cups coconut milk
1 teaspoon salt
4 cardamoms, crushed
10 almonds, blanched and chopped
10 cashew nuts, chopped

Wash the rice, soak and leave to drain. Heat ghee and fry the onions and curry leaves. Keep some onion back for garnishing. Add the drained rice and fry till the rice becomes opaque. Add the peppercorns, cloves, turmeric, coconut milk and salt. Bring to the boil, cover and simmer gently. When the rice is nearly cooked, stir in the crushed cardamoms. Fry the nuts and onion for a garnish. This recipe is from South India.

Kashmiri Pulau

Kashmiri cooking has a Middle Eastern flavour and the cuisine centres around meat preparations. Here is an unusual sweet and sour pulau using only vegetables.

1½ cups rice
10 oz (280 g) vegetables, cubed
1 inch (2·5 cm) piece ginger, finely chopped
2 teaspoons coriander seeds
1 inch (2·5 cm) piece cinnamon, broken
2 teaspoons salt
1 tablespoon soft brown sugar

juice of 1½ lemons
2 tablespoons ghee
6 cloves
8 peppercorns
3 green cardamoms
20 almonds, blanched and chopped
¾ teaspoon saffron, pounded in a little warm milk

Wash the rice and leave to soak. Wash the vegetables and put in a saucepan with 2 cups of boiling water. Add ginger, coriander, cinnamon, a teaspoon of salt and cook till tender. Add sugar, juice of 1 lemon and heat till the sugar has dissolved. Meanwhile, boil the rice, adding the rest of the lemon juice, in a separate pan till half-cooked. Drain. Heat ghee and fry the cloves, peppercorns and cardamoms. Add the rice, vegetables and stock, almonds and saffron milk. Mix well and cook gently till all the liquid is absorbed and the rice is cooked. Serve with a savoury dish.

Savoury Pulau with Nuts

This rich pulau is based on one introduced by the Mughals. The rice is first cooked and then served in layers on top of a nut and onion garnish.

For the pulau:

1½ cups rice
2 tablespoons ghee
1 onion, chopped
6 cloves garlic, finely chopped
12 peppercorns
6 cloves
4 green cardamoms
1 inch (2·5 cm) piece of cinnamon, broken

2 green chillies, chopped (optional)
1½ teaspoons salt
½ teaspoon cumin seeds
1 inch (2·5 cm) piece ginger, finely chopped

For mixing with the cooked pulau:

⅓ cup cooked peas
2 tomatoes, sliced
½ teaspoon garam masala

⅓ cup fried panir cubes
½ teaspoon paprika or chilli
    powder

Wash and soak the rice for ½ hour in water. Drain. Heat ghee and fry the onion and garlic. Stir in the peppercorns, cloves, cardamoms, cinnamon and chillies. Add rice. Stir in salt, cumin seeds and ginger and fry till the rice becomes opaque. Add 3 cups of hot water, bring to the boil, cover and simmer gently till cooked. Meanwhile prepare the garnish base from these ingredients:

2 onions, sliced
2 tablespoons ghee
20 almonds, blanched
20 cashew nuts
1 tablespoon pistachio nuts
1 inch (2·5 cm) piece ginger,
    finely chopped

2 tablespoons sultanas
2 green chillies, finely sliced
    (optional)
2 hard-boiled eggs (optional)
chopped coriander leaf

Heat ghee and fry the onions till they begin to turn golden. Stir in the nuts, ginger, sultanas and chillies and fry for a few minutes. Chop the eggs and sprinkle with a little salt, paprika and garam masala. Mix the garnish and divide in 3 parts. Divide the cooked rice in 3 parts and add the peas, tomatoes and panir cubes to one part respectively. Spread one part of the garnish on the centre of the serving dish. Cover with the peas and rice. Spread the second layer of garnish over this and cover with the panir and rice. Spread the third layer of garnish and cover with the tomatoes and rice. Finally sprinkle with chopped coriander leaves and serve with a curry.

Aubergine Pulau (*Vangī Bāth*)

In this South Indian pulau, the aubergine is prepared in a special masala before being added to the cooked rice.

1½ cups rice
2 tablespoons ghee
1 onion, chopped
4 cloves
2 green cardamoms

1 inch (2·5 cm) piece
    cinnamon, broken
1½ teaspoons salt
10 oz (280 g) aubergines
1 teaspoon mustard seeds
½ teaspoon turmeric powder

For the masala:

1 tablespoon grated coconut
6 peppercorns
1 teaspoon coriander seeds
1 teaspoon yellow (channa) dal

1 teaspoon black (urhad) dal
½ teaspoon paprika or chilli
  powder

Wash the rice, soak and drain. Heat ghee and lightly fry the onions, cloves, cardamoms and cinnamon. Add the drained rice and fry till the rice becomes opaque. Add salt and 3 cups of hot water, bring to the boil, turn down the heat and simmer till the rice is cooked. Meanwhile, slice the aubergines and leave to soak in water. Grind the masala ingredients and fry for a few minutes in ghee. In a separate pan, fry the mustard seeds gently till they begin to jump, then add the aubergine slices, turmeric and ½ teaspoon salt. Fry till the slices are tender and stir in the fried masala. Add to the cooked pulau and mix well. Serve hot with lemon slices and yogurt.

Beetroot Rice (*Chukunda chāval*)

1½ cups rice
2 tablespoons ghee
1 teaspoon mustard seeds
1 teaspoon ground black
  pepper
¼ teaspoon cumin seeds
1 tablespoon gram dal
1 tablespoon black (urhad) dal
2 green chillies, chopped
  (optional)

2 onions, chopped
a few curry leaves
1 large cooked beetroot, diced
½ teaspoon salt
¼ teaspoon turmeric powder
juice of 1 lemon
10 cashew nuts, chopped

Boil the washed rice with a teaspoon of salt, drain and keep warm. Heat 2 tablespoons of ghee and fry the mustard seeds, pepper, cumin seeds, dals and chillies. Add onions and curry leaves and fry till the onion begins to turn golden. Stir in the beetroot, salt and turmeric and fry for a few minutes. Mix well with the cooked rice and sprinkle with lemon juice. Garnish with fried cashew nuts and serve hot with yogurt.

Peach Rice (*Arū chāval*)

2 cups rice
2 tablespoons ghee
1 dessertspoon mustard seeds
1 dessertspoon black (urhad) dal
½ teaspoon paprika or chilli powder

1 cup grated coconut
1 lb (450 g) peaches, sliced
½ teaspoon turmeric powder
10 cashew nuts, chopped
1 dessertspoon sultanas
a few curry leaves
1 teaspoon salt

Wash the rice, boil, drain and keep hot. Heat ghee and fry the mustard seeds, dal and paprika. Add coconut and peaches and fry for 5 minutes. Add turmeric, cashew nuts, sultanas, curry leaves and salt and fry for a few more minutes. Stir into the cooked rice, mix well and serve hot with chutney.

Saffron Rice and Panir

1½ cups rice
1 teaspoon salt
pinch of saffron
1 dessertspoon wholewheat flour (ata)
4 oz (113 g) panir cubes
ghee for frying
2 green cardamoms, ground seeds

1 cup yogurt
4 oz (113 g) cooked peas
½ teaspoon garam masala
½ teaspoon paprika or chilli powder
½ teaspoon cumin seeds

For the garnish:

1 inch (2·5 cm) piece ginger, finely chopped
1 onion, chopped

cucumber slices
chopped fresh coriander leaf

Wash the rice, boil with a teaspoon of salt and drain. Dissolve a good pinch of saffron in a cup of warm milk and stir half into the rice to make it yellow. While the rice is boiling make a batter of flour, a pinch of salt and water. Dip the panir cubes in the batter and fry till golden Remove from the ghee. Add the ground cardamom seeds to the rest of the saffron milk and beat into the yogurt. Leave the fried panir to soak in this mixture. Stir the peas into the rice and divide into two parts. Spread one part in a pan or casserole and sprinkle with half the garam masala, paprika and cumin seeds. Cover with half the panir mixture. Now add the second portion of rice. Sprinkle on the rest of the garam masala, paprika and cumin seeds, cover with the rest of the panir mixture. Heat through and serve garnished with fried onion and ginger, sliced cucumber and chopped fresh coriander leaf. Serve with a curry and yogurt.

Rice and Lentils (*Khichharī*)

Captain Alexander Hamilton, who was in India and the East Indies from 1688–1723, noted in his journal that the famous Mughal emperor, Aurangzeb, was particularly fond of Khichhari. Its strengthening powers were appreciated by European sailors of the time who used to eat it once or twice a week on 'Banian Days'.

Khichhari must be carefully cooked to avoid becoming the mushy dish known in English as Kegderee. When khichhari is served as dry as possible, it may be known as *bhūnī khichharī*. The more moist dish given to children and invalids is known as *gīlī khichharī*.

1 cup green (mung) dal or lentils	$\frac{1}{2}$ teaspoon garam masala
1 cup rice	2 tablespoons ghee
1 tablespoon chopped fresh coriander leaves	1 onion, finely chopped
1 inch (2.5 cm) piece ginger	$\frac{1}{2}$ teaspoon cumin seeds
4 cloves garlic	2 green chillies, finely chopped (optional)
$\frac{1}{2}$ teaspoon turmeric powder	2 tomatoes, quartered
$\frac{1}{2}$ teaspoon paprika or chilli powder	1 potato, diced
	1 teaspoon salt

Soak the dal beforehand. Wash and drain the rice. Pound the coriander leaves, ginger and garlic with turmeric, paprika and garam masala in a mortar. Heat ghee and lightly fry the onion, stir in the masala paste with the cumin seeds and green chillies. Fry for a few minutes and add the rice, dal and tomatoes. Fry for a further five minutes and cover with water. Add the potato pieces and salt and bring to the boil. Lower heat and simmer till the rice is cooled. Add extra water if necessary to avoid drying up. Serve sprinkled with chopped coriander leaves.

Bengali Khichhari

Use 2 parts rice to 1 part of lentils or mung dal. Ghee may be added to give extra body. Flavour with a little spice and chopped onions.

Gujerati Khichhari

The seventeenth-century Portuguese traveller, Sebastian Manrique, who visited India during the reign of Shahjahan, noted that on festive occasions Bengalis ate a rich and costly dish called Gujerati khichhari. Here is a recipe containing the essential ingredients:

$\frac{3}{4}$ cup lentils or green (mung) dal
$1\frac{1}{2}$ cups rice
4 cloves
2 inches (5 cm) cinnamon, broken
4 cardamoms
$1\frac{1}{2}$ teaspoons salt
$\frac{1}{2}$ teaspoon turmeric powder
3 tablespoons ghee
1 onion, sliced

1 dessertspoon mustard seed
10 almonds, blanched
10 cashew nuts
1 tablespoon raisins
$\frac{1}{2}$ teaspoon nutmeg, grated
$\frac{1}{2}$ teaspoon mace
$\frac{1}{2}$ teaspoon black pepper, ground
1 teaspoon cumin seed
1 teaspoon coriander powder

Soak the dal beforehand. Wash the rice and cook with the dal in water with cloves, cinnamon, cardamom, salt and turmeric. Drain when cooked. Meanwhile heat ghee and lightly fry the onion and mustard seed, add nuts, raisins, nutmeg, mace, pepper, cumin seed and coriander. Fry for a few minutes till the nuts are browned then stir into the cooked rice and dal. Mix well. Extra ghee can be added according to taste. Serve hot with a pickle or curry.

South Indian Khichhari (*Ven pongal*)

1 cup green (mung) dal
2 cups rice
1 teaspoon peppercorns
2 teaspoons cumin seeds
1 inch (2·5 cm) piece of ginger,
  finely chopped

2 teaspoons salt
4 tablespoons ghee
2 tablespoons cashew nuts

Soak the dal and boil the rice and dal together with the peppercorns, cumin, ginger and salt. Heat ghee and fry the nuts till golden. Pour into the khichhari and mix thoroughly. Serve with coconut chutney, *Avial* or potato chutney.

Savoury Sesame Rice (*Puli chorai*)

South Indian food tends to be quite hot. This dish is made hotter by adding up to 16 or more red chillies.

2 cups rice
2 teaspoons salt
4 tablespoons sesame (til) oil
1 teaspoon fenugreek (methi)
  seeds
1 teaspoon turmeric powder
1 teaspoon paprika or chilli
  powder

1 tablespoon gram dal
2 teaspoons black (urhad) dal
2 teaspoons sesame seeds
2 teaspoons coriander seeds
1 tablespoon peanuts
2 teaspoons mustard seeds
a few curry leaves
juice of 1 lemon

Boil the rice with salt and drain. Sprinkle with 2 tablespoons sesame oil. Fry the fenugreek seeds, turmeric, paprika, dals, sesame seeds and coriander seeds in a tablespoon of sesame oil for 5 minutes and mix with the rice. Fry the nuts, mustard seeds and curry leaves till the nuts turn golden and add the rice. Sprinkle with lemon juice and mix thoroughly. Serve with fried papads and Avial.

Rice and Curd *(Dahibāth)*

2 cups rice
2 teaspoons salt
1 tablespoon ghee
2 teaspoons mustard seeds
1 tablespoon black (urhad) dal
4 cups yogurt
3-4 green chillies, chopped
  (optional)

1 inch (2·5 cm) piece ginger,
  finely chopped
1 small mango, sliced
  (if available)
½ teaspoon salt

Boil the rice with salt, drain and keep warm. Heat ghee and fry the
mustard seeds and dal and beat into the yogurt. Stir in the chillies,
ginger and mango. Add salt and mix thoroughly with the rice.
Serve with lime pickle or curry.

Rice Balls *(Kadāmbuttū)*

2 cups rice
2 teaspoons salt

3 tablespoons coconut, finely
  grated
ghee

Wash the rice, drain and crush coarsely. Add the crushed rice to
5 cups of salted boiling water. Cook till the mixture is thick, stirring
to prevent lumps forming. Remove from the heat, stir in the coconut
and leave to cool. Grease the hands and roll the mixture into egg-
sized balls and wrap in a muslin cloth. Steam for about half an hour
till the balls are light and tender. Serve hot with curry or pickles.

Breads Pancakes and Dumplings

Many of these recipes involve the preparation of a dough. A few precautions will ensure that your results are successful. Atmospheric conditions change and you may find that more flour is needed on damper days. If your dough still sticks to the bowl or your hands after adding all the ingredients, keep kneading and adding a little flour at a time until the ball of dough comes away clean. Always knead well till your dough is soft and pliable. Some doughs acquire a silky texture when ready. If the dough contains yeast, be careful not to leave it too long over the stated period since the effect of the yeast will be lost in cooking. When leaving a dough to stand, cover with a damp cloth.

Unleavened Wholewheat Bread
(Chapātis and Phulkas)

Phulkas are small chapatis. Elephants are commonly fed chapatis the size of motor wheels. Most of the princely states used to keep elephants for ceremonial purposes as well as for work. I have heard of a certain elephant who was in the habit of weighing his chapatis with his trunk. If one turned out to be underweight, the offending chapati was contemptuously flung away. In the same state was an elephant who was very fond of his driver (*mahut*). He demonstrated this affection by always leaving aside a portion of his vegetable and chapati for the beloved mahut.

For 10–15 chapatis make a flour and water dough with 2 cups of wholewheat flour (*ātā*). Sift the flour with a teaspoon of salt and add water gradually, mixing until a soft dough is formed. Knead well with the fist, folding and kneading the dough till it is really pliable. Sprinkle with drops of water, cover with a damp cloth and leave to stand for a minimum of 30 minutes. Set the tava (iron hot-plate) on a medium heat to warm up, slightly greased. Before cooking, knead the dough again, break off pellets and roll into walnut-sized balls. Flatten between the fingers, dip in flour and roll out thinly and evenly on a floured board. Experts flatten them with a few vigorous slaps between the palms. Put the chapati on the tava. When it is well heated through, the edges begin to turn up. This is the time to turn it over and bake the other side. When the chapati begins to appear bubbly (the water inside is trying to escape as steam and bubbles up the dough) remove it from the tava and hold over a gas flame, a hot electric ring or under the grill. The chapati should now puff up completely like a ball. As it collapses, transfer to a plate covered with a clean cloth. The whole process should not take more than half a minute. Try to establish a rhythm of work so that you are rolling out the next chapati while another one is baking.

Chapatis are eaten with curries. You can tear off pieces and use them like a spoon. They are ideal for mopping up gravy or sauce. Warm chapatis and butter are excellent for breakfast or tea and I have yet to meet a child who does not relish them with jam or honey.

Buttered Wholewheat Unleavened Bread (Pārathas)

2 cups wholewheat flour (ata)
about 1 cup water

$\frac{1}{2}$ teaspoon salt
ghee

Prepare the dough as for chapatis and leave to stand. Put the tava on to warm. Heat the ghee and have some liquid ghee available. Roll out balls of dough using a little dry flour, not too thinly. Spread a spoonful of ghee over, fold over, roll and spread on more ghee. Do this two or three times and finally roll out fairly thin. Grease the tava and bake one side of the paratha. Grease the top and turn to cook the other side. Turn again if necessary to complete the cooking. Parathas take longer than chapatis and care must be taken not to burn them.

A particular paratha is made in Bengal from a plain flour (maida) dough. When the ghee is spread on the uncooked circular parātha, a cut is made with a knife from the centre outwards. Using this cut, the parātha is rolled into a cone which is then squashed flat. The plain flour parātha has a heavier texture.

Stuffed Parāthas

Make up the dough as for parathas.

For the stuffing:

2 potatoes
1 tablespoon ghee
1 onion, finely chopped
2 tablespoons coriander leaf
  or fresh herbs, finely
  chopped

$\frac{1}{2}$ inch (15 mm) piece ginger,
  finely chopped
1 teaspoon salt
$\frac{1}{2}$ teaspoon garam masala
$\frac{1}{4}$ teaspoon chilli powder
1 dessertspoon lemon juice

Boil the potatoes and when cool, peel and mash. Heat ghee and fry the onion, herbs and ginger for a few minutes. Add salt, garam masala and chilli powder. Mix in the mashed potato and sprinkle with lemon juice. Fry for 2 minutes and allow to cool. Roll out the paratha not too thin, spread on ghee and place a tablespoon of stuffing in the centre. Fold up and gently roll out as thin as possible, using a little dry flour. Cook in the usual way. Serve with a curry or yogurt (*dahi*).

Other combinations of vegetables can be used as a stuffing. Substitute 8 oz (225 g) frozen peas and a chopped tomato for the potatoes, for example.

Sweet Lentil Parātha (*Channa dāl parātha*)

$1\frac{1}{4}$ cups split gram (channa dal)
2 cups wholewheat flour (ata)
$\frac{1}{2}$ teaspoon salt

1 cup sugar
2 cloves, ground
2 cardamoms, ground seeds

Wash and soak the lentils. Make up the paratha dough and leave to stand. Boil the lentils till soft and mash. Stir in the sugar, cloves and cardamom. Roll out the parathas and place some filling in the centre. Fold up and roll out as thin as possible. Bake in the usual way. Serve hot with yogurt or spread with butter.

This lentil paratha can be made savoury by substituting 1 teaspoon salt, $\frac{1}{2}$ teaspoon cumin powder, $\frac{1}{2}$ teaspoon paprika or chilli powder for the sugar. These are sometimes known as *dāl bhari pūris*.

Puffed Fried Bread (*Pūris and Lūchchis*)
For puris:

2 cups wholewheat flour (ata)
2 tablespoons ghee

$\frac{1}{2}$ teaspoon salt
ghee for deep-frying

Rub the ghee into the flour and salt. Gradually mix in enough water to make a stiff dough. Knead well and make up into small ping-pong-size balls. Heat ghee in a small saucepan to nearly smoking point. Turn the heat down to medium. Lightly grease the rolling board and roller. Flatten a dough ball, dip quickly in the hot ghee and roll out thinly on the board. Make sure that the puri is not bigger than the pan. Drop it in the hot ghee and press gently with the back of a spoon. The puri should immediately puff up like a ball. Allow to turn golden, turn and quickly fry the other side.

As in making chapatis, the cooking should be done quickly. A rhythm of work can be established so that you are dipping and rolling out the next puri while the other is browning in the hot ghee. Puris are eaten with most dishes, especially semolina (*sūji*), kabli channas and dry curries.

For luchchis:

Luchchis are fried breads like puris but plain flour (*maida*) is used to make the dough. They are a favourite in Bengal. Proceed as for puris, frying one at a time in hot ghee.

Sesame Pūris (*Til pūri*)

2 cups plain flour (maida)
1½ teaspoons sesame seeds
½ teaspoon salt
½ teaspoon soft brown sugar

1 teaspoon caraway seeds
1 teaspoon crushed black
  peppercorns
ghee for deep-frying

Sieve the flour and mix all the ingredients. Add warm water gradually to make a stiff dough. Knead well. Roll out to make thin round puris. Deep fry in hot ghee till golden.

Banana Pūris (*Kela pūri*)

2 cups plain flour (maida)
1 cup gram flour (besan)
½ teaspoon paprika or chilli
  powder
½ teaspoon turmeric powder
½ teaspoon cumin seeds

1 teaspoon salt
1 tablespoon ghee
4 ripe bananas
1 teaspoon soft brown sugar
ghee for deep-frying

Sieve the flour and mix in the paprika, turmeric, cumin and salt. Rub in a tablespoon of ghee and knead well. Mash the bananas. Stir in the sugar and add to the flour. Knead make a to dough, adding a little warm water if necessary. Make into small balls and roll out to form thin puris. Deep-fry in hot ghee till golden. This puri may also be baked on a tava (iron hot-plate) smeared with a little ghee.

Leavened Pūris (*Khamīri pūri*)

These breads, sometimes called *nāns*, and are served covered with silver leaf (*varak*) if this is available.

2 cups plain flour (maida)
2 tablespoons Khamir yeast (see below)
3 teaspoons sugar

1 teaspoon salt
2 tablespoons ghee
1 cup warm milk
1 egg, beaten (optional)

For the Khamir yeast:

1 cup plain flour (maida)
2 tablespoons warm yogurt
2 teaspoons sugar

12 black peppercorns
2 tablespoons warm water

Mix the Khamir ingredients, beat well and leave in a warm place overnight. Remove peppercorns before use.

Sieve the flour, add the khamir, sugar, salt and ghee. Gradually add warm milk and egg to make a dough. Knead well and leave to stand for two hours. Sprinkle on a little warm water and knead again. Roll out as puris and leave to rise again. Deep-fry in hot ghee. Serve with bhujia or curry.

Leavened Bread (*Khamīri roti*)

Any *khamir* left over can be used to make leavened bread (*khamiri roti*). Sift 4 cups of wholewheat or plain flour. Add the yeast and 2 teaspoons of salt. Gradually mix in warm water to make a dough. Knead well. Cover and leave in a warm place to rise. When the dough is nearly double its original size make about 6 round, flat and thick rotis with the palm of the hand, using a little dry flour. Bake on both sides on the tava, finish under the grill. The roti can be deep-fried in hot ghee if preferred, like a *bhatūra*.

Flat Baked Bread (*Nān*)

Emperor Akbar's prime minister, Abul Fazl, compiled an account of the administrative and revenue systems of the time, called the Aiin-i-

Akbari. In it is recorded the largest kind of bread to be baked in the royal kitchen. This mighty nan was made of 10 seers (20 lbs/9 kilos) of maida (plain fine wheat flour), 5 seers of cow's milk, 1½ seers of ghee and ¼ seer of salt. The smallest nan can be made using these proportions.

2 cups wholewheat or plain
   flour
½ teaspoon salt

1 tablespoon ghee
5 oz (140 ml) milk

Sift the flour with the salt and rub in the ghee. Gradually mix in the milk and enough water to make a soft dough. Form into flat cakes about 12 inches (30 cm) across and ¼ inch (6 mm) thick. Bake in a hot oven till light brown and crisp.

Gram Flour Bread (*Besan roti*)

2 cups gram flour (besan)
1 small onion, finely chopped
¼ teaspoon chilli powder

½ teaspoon cumin seeds
½ teaspoon salt
1 tablespoon ghee

Mix the flour with the onion, chilli, cumin and salt. Rub in the ghee. Add enough water to make a stiff dough. Divide into balls and roll out as for parathas but not too thin so that the onion breaks through Heat the tava (iron hot-plate) to medium heat and lightly grease with ghee. Brown both sides of the roti. Serve with a curry or yogurt.

Plain Flour Leavened Bread (*Shīrmāl, Roghni nān*)

1 cup yogurt
1 cup milk
½ teaspoon baking powder
2 eggs, lightly beaten
1 tablespoon ghee, melted
5½–6½ cups plain flour (maida)

1 teaspoon salt
6 green cardamoms, ground
   seeds (optional)
1 teaspoon sugar
1 tablespoon dried yeast or
   khamir

Beat the yogurt, warm gently in a pan and stir in the milk, baking powder, eggs and melted ghee. Sift together the flour, salt, cardamom powder, sugar and yeast. Work in the yogurt mixture gradually till a stiff dough is formed. Knead well for at least 15 minutes. Cover and leave in a warm place till the dough has risen to nearly twice its original size (2 hours). Knead again. Break into 8 large balls and shape into flat, oval nans about 10 inches (25 cm) across and of pancake thickness, with the help of a little dry flour. Brush the top with warm milk and melted butter. Bake in a hot oven for 10–15 minutes on a greased dish. When ready the nans should be soft and light gold. They can also be cooked on a tava (iron hot-plate) by baking on both sides. On special occasions they can be sprinkled with sesame seeds and poppy seeds before baking. Serve hot with dal, a curry, rabarhi or khir.

These nans are relished at teatime, slit in half and spread with butter. They are ideal for stuffing. Make a slit in the side and fill with chopped and seasoned salad or some vegetables cooked in a savoury sauce. Wholewheat flour may be substituted for plain flour to increase the nourishment.

Wholewheat Leavened Bread *(Bhatūra)*

2 cups wholewheat flour (ata)   ½ teaspoon baking powder
½ teaspoon salt   1 teaspoon sugar (optional)

Sift the flour with the salt, baking powder and sugar. Mix in enough warm water or yogurt to make a stiff dough (about 5 fl. oz (140 ml)), knead well. Cover and leave in a warm place to rise for about 4 hours. Knead again. Shape into small balls and flatten to form thick pancakes about 5 inches (12 cm) across. Deep-fry in ghee or bake on both sides on a hot tava. The bhaturas should puff up. Serve with Kabli channas or potato curry and chutney.

Spicy Pancakes *(Dosa)*

These South Indian pancakes are served for breakfast. They can be prepared from a variety of flours. Experiment will enable you to find your favourite combination.

2 cups rice flour   ½ teaspoon brown sugar
3 tablespoons split black pea   ¼ teaspoon baking powder
  flour (urhad)   3 green chillies, finely chopped
1 teaspoon salt   (optional)

Mix the ingredients well and beat in enough water to form a pancake batter. Stand in a warm place for half an hour. Heat a tava or heavy frying pan, wipe with ghee and fry 2 spoonfuls of batter like an English pancake. Serve with yogurt and chutney. A filling may be prepared using the following ingredients:

12 oz (340 g) potatoes
1 tablespoon grated coconut
2–4 green chillies, chopped
  (optional)
1 inch (2·5 cm) ginger
1 tablespoon ghee
1 onion, finely chopped

1½ teaspoons split black peas
  (urhad dal)
1½ teaspoons split gram
  (channa dal)
1 teaspoon mustard seeds
½ teaspoon cumin powder
½ teaspoon turmeric powder

Boil the potatoes, peel and mash. Grind the coconut, chillies, ginger and a few drops of water to a paste. Heat ghee and fry the onion. Add the dals, mustard seeds, cumin and turmeric and stir-fry for a few minutes. Add potato and masala paste and continue frying for 5 minutes. Put a portion of the filling in the centre of each pancake and fold. Put a little ghee on the sides of the pan, turn the dosa and fry till crisp.

The batter can be changed by mixing 1 cup of rice flour with 1 cup mixed dal flours. A semolina batter can be made for this masala dosa. Mix 2 cups of semolina with 3 teaspoons of yogurt, ½ teaspoon baking powder, ½ teaspoon salt and enough water to make a creamy batter. Leave to stand for a few hours and use as above.

Oat Pancake (*Diliya dosa*)

8 oz (225 g) rolled oats
2 cups yogurt
2 green chillies, finely chopped
  (optional)
1 onion, finely chopped

½ inch (15 mm) piece of ginger,
  finely chopped
½ teaspoon salt
ghee for frying

Mix the ingredients to a thick batter. Heat a dessertspoon of ghee in a heavy frying pan and drop in tablespoons of batter to make thin pancakes, browning on both sides. Serve hot with curry, pickles or dal.

Coconut Pancake (*Narial dosa*)

2 cups rice flour
2 cups fresh coconut, finely
  grated
1 inch (2·5 cm) piece ginger,
  chopped
2 green chillies, chopped
  (optional)

2 onions, finely chopped
1 dessertspoon chopped fresh
  coriander leaves
a few curry leaves
1 teaspoon salt

Mix the rice flour, coconut, ginger and chillies and grind. Mix to a smooth paste by adding water gradually. Lightly fry the onion and stir into the paste along with the coriander, curry leaves and salt. Add enough water to make a thick batter. Cook to make dosas.

Wholewheat Pancake (*Āṭā dosa*)

2 cups wholewheat flour (ata)
2 onions, finely chopped
2 green chillies, finely chopped
  (optional)
1 teaspoon chopped coriander
  leaves

a few curry leaves
pinch of salt
pinch of baking powder

Mix the flour, onion, chillies and herbs. Add salt and baking powder and enough water to make a thick, creamy batter. Cook to make dosas. Serve hot with chutney, yogurt or curry.

Semolina Dumplings (*Sūji idli*)

1 lb (450 g) semolina
8 oz (225 g) vermicelli
6 tablespoons ghee
1 tablespoon mustard seeds
1 tablespoon split black peas
  (urhad dal)
$\frac{1}{2}$ teaspoon chilli powder

10 cashew nuts, chopped
a few curry leaves
2 cups yogurt
1 inch (2·5 cm) piece ginger,
  finely chopped
1 teaspoon salt

Lightly fry the semolina and vermicelli in half the ghee without browning. Leave to cool. Heat the rest of the ghee and fry the mustard seeds, dal, chilli, nuts and curry leaves till the nuts are golden. Beat the yogurt till smooth and mix in the semolina and vermicelli. Add the fried spices, ginger and salt. Add enough water to make a very thick batter. Mix well and leave to stand for about half an hour. Pour the batter into small, heat-resistant bowls, cover and steam. The idlis are cooked when a dry fork can be pulled out clean (about 15 minutes). Serve hot with a green chutney or curry.

Gram Flour Crispy Wafers (*Pappadams*)

Papads can be bought made up in packets in supermarkets and Asian stores. They should be rapidly deep-fried in hot ghee or oil, drained and eaten as soon as possible. Do not allow to burn or blacken as this spoils the taste. There are many varieties of size and contents and it is worth experimenting to find the type you prefer.

Legumes

'They have several Species of Lagumen; but those of Doll are most in use.' (Captain Alexander Hamilton, *New Account of the East Indies* Volume 1, 1725).

In India, the legume family supplies a number of peas and beans which are used fresh or dried. Dried legumes are stored whole or split. When split they are called *dāl*. They are boiled to make a thick sauce which functions in a similar way to the gravy of Western dishes. They are also used in sweets and cutlets. Gram flour is used in batters, pancakes and chapatis. The legumes are rich in protein and any legume dish will provide really nourishing food.

Split Black Peas *(Urhad dāl)*

2 cups split black peas
  (urhad dal)

1 inch (2·5 cm) piece ginger
1 clove garlic

2 green chillies, chopped (optional)
½ teaspoon paprika or chilli powder
1 teaspoon turmeric powder

2 tablespoons ghee
2 onions, chopped
8 oz (225 g) tomatoes, chopped
1½ teaspoons salt
1 teaspoon garam masala

Wash the dal and allow to soak for a while. Grind together the ginger, chilli and turmeric, adding a few drops of water to make a thick paste. Heat ghee and fry the onion. Stir in the paste and fry for a few minutes then add the tomato and drained dal. Allow to sizzle, cover with water, add salt and allow to cook till tender. Before serving, stir in the garam masala and a knob of butter or ghee.

In the Panjab this dish is often enriched by cooking the dal in milk. Allow to get tender before adding the masala. Serve hot with breads or rice.

Split yellow Gram *(Channa dāl)*

Use the recipe for urhad dal in the same proportions.

Spiced Gram *(Amti)*

1 cup yellow split peas (channa dal)
2 tablespoons ghee
½ teaspoon mustard seeds
3 green chillies, chopped (optional)
1 onion, finely chopped
½ teaspoon turmeric powder

½ teaspoon paprika or chilli powder
12 black peppercorns, crushed
1 inch (2·5 cm) piece of cinnamon, broken
4 cloves, crushed
2 green cardamoms, crushed
1 tablespoon lemon juice
1 teaspoon salt

Soak the dal for an hour. Drain and boil till soft. Heat ghee and fry the mustard seeds till they sputter. Add green chillies and onion and fry till golden. Stir in the turmeric and paprika. Crush the peppercorns, cinnamon, cloves and cardamom in a mortar and add to the pan. Fry for 2 minutes. Stir this mixture into the dal. Add lemon juice and salt, mix well and simmer. Serve hot with a curry.

Split Green Peas *(Mūng dāl)*

An ancient restorative for the aged makes use of this nourishing dal. Steep the washed dal in milk and sugar or honey and leave in a warm place for a few hours. Remove the dal, grind to a paste, make into little cakes and fry in ghee. Here is a recipe for use with curry or chapatis:

1 cup split green peas (mung dal)	2 cloves garlic, finely chopped
1 teaspoon salt	1 inch (2·5 cm) piece ginger, finely chopped
½ teaspoon turmeric powder	½ teaspoon cumin seeds
2 tablespoons ghee	1 teaspoon coriander powder
2 onions, chopped	chopped coriander leaf

Wash the dal and leave to soak for an hour. Drain and boil in a little water with salt and turmeric till soft. Meanwhile, heat ghee and fry the onion, garlic and ginger till golden. Stir in the cumin and coriander powder and fry for a few minutes. Add to the dal a few minutes before it is ready. Serve hot garnished with chopped coriander leaf.

Red Lentils *(Masūr dāl)*

Any of the previous dal recipes may be used with masur dal but the following two recipes make tasty alternatives:

Masur Dal 1

1 cup red lentils	6 cloves
1 teaspoon cumin seeds	2 inch (5 cm) piece cinnamon
1 teaspoon poppy seeds	4 green cardamoms
1 teaspoon paprika or chilli powder	1 cup grated coconut
1 teaspoon turmeric powder	4 black peppercorns
1 teaspoon salt	4 cloves garlic
2 teaspoons coriander seeds	2 tablespoons ghee
	2 onions, chopped

Wash the dal and leave to soak for an hour. Drain and bring to the boil with salt in a little water. Cook on a medium heat. Meanwhile grind all the ingredients except the onions and salt. Heat ghee and fry the onions till golden. Add the masala paste and fry for a few minutes. Stir into the dal just before it is ready. Serve hot with rice and curry.

Masur Dal 2

1 cup red lentils	2 green chillies (optional)
½ teaspoon turmeric powder	2 tablespoons ghee
1 teaspoon salt	4 cloves garlic, finely chopped
1 teaspoon cumin powder	1 onion, chopped
2 potatoes, chopped	1 teaspoon garam masala
4 tomatoes, chopped	
1 tablespoon chopped coriander leaves	

Wash the dal, soak, drain and boil in 5 cups water, adding turmeric, salt and cumin together with the potatoes and tomatoes. When the potatoes are cooked, add the coriander leaves and green chillies. Heat ghee and fry the garlic and onion till golden. Stir in the garam masala and fry for two minutes. Add to the dal, mix well and serve hot with rice.

Split Tuvar Peas *(Tūr dāl)*

This dal comes from Madras in South India and is usually made hot with plenty of chillies.

1½ cups tur dal	juice of half a lemon or tamarind juice
pinch of saffron	
2 tablespoons ghee	1 teaspoon sambhar masala
1 teaspoon mustard seeds	2 teaspoons salt
a few curry leaves	green chillies to taste

Wash the dal, soak and boil till soft with saffron and a tablespoon of ghee. Meanwhile fry mustard seeds and curry leaves in a tablespoon of ghee for a few minutes. Add sambhar masala and salt to the lemon juice and stir into the fried mixture. Pour into the dal and mix well. Add a few green chillies to taste. Serve hot with curry and rice.

Tuvar Peas and Plums

1½ cups split tuvar peas (tur dal)	6–8 unripe plums, stoned and halved
½ teaspoon salt	1 tablespoon ghee

1 onion, chopped
2 cloves garlic, finely chopped
1 teaspoon turmeric powder
1 teaspoon mustard seeds

½ teaspoon paprika or chilli
    powder
a few curry leaves

Wash, soak and drain the dal. Boil in salted water. When nearly tender add the plum pieces. Heat ghee and fry the onion and garlic till golden. Add the spices and fry for a few minutes. Stir into the dal. Serve hot with rice.

Lentils and Spinach *(Dāl sāg)*

1½ cups mixed dals
1 lb (450 g) spinach
½ teaspoon turmeric powder
1 teaspoon salt
½ teaspoon paprika or chilli
    powder

2 tablespoons ghee
1 onion, chopped
1 teaspoon mustard seeds
½ teaspoon cumin seeds
1 teaspoon garam masala

Wash the dal and leave to soak. Wash the spinach and chop finely. Boil 3 cups of water and add the drained dal, turmeric, salt and paprika. Cook for 5 minutes and add the spinach. Keep on a medium heat till most of the moisture has gone. Meanwhile heat ghee and fry the onions, mustard seeds and cumin seeds till golden. Stir into the dal and spinach with a teaspoon of garam masala. Keep on a moderate heat till cooked. The dish is dry but add a little water to prevent catching. Serve hot with rice.

Hot Lentils *(Sambhar)*

1 cup dal
2 carrots, chopped
2 potatoes, chopped
1½ teaspoons salt
2 teaspoons turmeric powder
1 oz (30 g) tamarind or juice of
    1 lemon
2 tablespoons ghee

1 teaspoon cumin powder
2 teaspoons coriander powder
½ cup grated coconut
1½ tablespoons mustard seeds
2 green chillies, chopped
    (optional)
10 curry leaves
2 teaspoons sambhar masala

Wash, soak and boil the lentils with carrots, potatoes, salt and turmeric in 3 cups water till tender. Meanwhile soak the tamarind
in half a cup of hot water and squeeze out the liquid. Add to the dal.
Heat ghee and fry the cumin, coriander and coconut. Add mustard
seeds, green chilli and curry leaves and fry for a few minutes. Add
sambhar masala, mix well and stir into the dal. Serve hot with dosas
or boiled rice.

This dish, like other dals, may be served as a soup or as a thicker
consistency according to taste.

Whole Black Peas (Urhad sabat)

1 cup whole black peas
4 cups water
2 teaspoons salt
1 teaspoon turmeric powder
1 inch (2·5 cm) piece ginger
$\frac{1}{2}$ teaspoon paprika or chilli
    powder

4 cloves garlic
2 green chillies, chopped
    (optional)
2 tablespoons chopped fresh
    coriander leaves
1 onion, chopped
2 tablespoons ghee

Wash the peas and leave them to soak. Boil the water and add the
peas, salt and tumeric. Grind the rest of the ingredients, except the
onion, to a paste. Heat ghee and gently fry the onion till golden.
Stir in the masala paste and add to the peas. Serve with chapatis
or plain rice.

Whole green peas (mung sabat) can be prepared in the same way.

Bengal Peas (Kabli channa)

1$\frac{1}{2}$ cups Bengal peas
1$\frac{1}{2}$ teaspoons salt
2 onions, finely chopped
1 green chilli, chopped
    optional)
1 inch (2·5 cm) piece ginger,
    finely chopped

2 green cardamoms
6 black peppercorns
1 inch (2·5 cm) piece
    cinnamon, broken
6 cloves
4 tablespoons ghee
4 cloves garlic, finely chopped

½ teaspoon paprika or chilli
   powder
1 teaspoon turmeric powder
½ teaspoon cumin powder
2 teaspoons coriander powder

1 tablespoon chopped
   coriander leaves
1 teaspoon garam masala
3 tablespoons lemon juice

For the garnish:

½ teaspoon cumin seed
2 chopped tomatoes

2 chopped cooked potatoes

Wash the whole channas and leave to soak in 3 cups water overnight.
Boil the following day with salt, half the onion, green chilli, ginger,
cardamoms, peppercorns, cinnamon and cloves. Simmer till tender.
Drain off the stock and keep. Heat ghee and fry the rest of the onion
and the garlic till golden. Add paprika, turmeric, cumin powder
and coriander powder. Add the drained channas and stir gently for
ten minutes. Mix in the coriander leaves, garam masala and lemon
juice. Now add as much stock as required for a gravy. Simmer gently.
Serve hot, sprinkled with a little cumin seed, chopped tomatoes and
potatoes. Serve with savoury rice or a vegetable dish. These channas
are excellent served cold with a salad. After boiling, drain and sprinkle
with lemon juice and paprika or chilli powder.

Bengal Peas and Curd (Dahi channa)

Stir 3 or more tablespoons of yogurt into the fried masala and channas.
Garnish as in the previous recipe and serve with bhaturas.

Gram Flour Curry (Besan kari)

This unusual mixed vegetable curry comes from the northwestern
state of Sind.

1 tablespoon tamarind or juice
   of half a lemon
2 tablespoons gram flour
   (besan)
3 tablespoons ghee
½ teaspoon paprika or chilli
   powder

2 green chillies, chopped
   (optional)
1 teaspoon fenugreek seeds
1 teaspoon cumin powder
2 teaspoons salt
1 potato, chopped
½ cup Lady Fingers (bhindi)

½ cup French beans, chopped
½ cup courgettes, chopped
2 carrots, chopped

2 tomatoes, chopped
10–12 curry leaves
1 tablespoon soft brown sugar

Soak the tamarind in half a cup of hot water and leave to soak. Mix the besan with a little water to make a paste. Add 4 more cups of water. Heat ghee in a saucepan and lightly fry the spices. Stir in the besan water and salt and continue cooking till half the liquid dries up. Add the vegetables and curry leaves and simmer till nearly tender. Stir in the brown sugar and tamarind water or lemon juice. Simmer till cooked and serve with plain rice.

Dal Cutlets (*Mongorhi*)

1 cup lentils
2 tablespoons ghee
1 small onion, finely chopped
1 tablespoon gram flour
  (besan)

1 teaspoon garam masala
1 teaspoon salt
1 dessertspoon yogurt

Wash and soak the dal overnight. Drain and grind to a paste. Heat ghee and fry the onion. Remove from the pan and fry the gram flour and garam masala for a few minutes. Mix all the ingredients and form into cutlets, using flour or breadcrumbs and fry in ghee till golden.

Turmeric or other spices such as bay leaf, cumin seed, ginger, may be added to this recipe. Mongorhis may be served as a hot or cold snack with yogurt or as a curry with pulau rice. An alternative method of making the dal paste is to cook the dal till soft and then mash.

The Tale of the Travellers

'It just goes to show how the obvious passes us by,' sighed the
guard. 'Yes, indeed,' the merchant mused. 'And how beautiful
the obvious seems to be on reflection, like the pristine purity of a
jewel.' He paused to chew on a clove. After offering some to his
companion he continued. 'I overlooked the obvious once, you know.'
'Really?' asked the guard, his eyebrows raised half hopefully, half
in surprise. 'Oh yes. But it was a long time ago now. I had just
set up shop in a small village. One day, just before dusk, three
travellers arrived. Straight away they made a fire, fetched water
from the village well and took out a large metal pot. Nothing
unusual about that, you might say. Some villagers had gathered to
watch, attracted by the cries of their children, and they were
amazed to see one of the travellers take some large, well-worn
pebbles from a bag, wash them carefully and drop them into the
pot. On enquiry, the travellers assured them that they were
masters at making Stone Curry, all they needed was a little ghee
and a few vegetables to give body to the flavour. Immediately the
villagers ran to their houses and returned with a few handfuls of
onions, carrots, potatoes and greens. The cook took the onions
and ghee and began to fry them in the pot, asking if by any chance
some kind person should have a little chilli and spices, just to bring
out the full flavour of the wonderful stones. These were then added
to the pot, the other vegetables were chopped nicely and thrown
in and finally a bowl of pure water was added. By now a crowd
had gathered and they sat down to watch and wait. Soon the cook
announced that the curry was ready and with a long ladle he
carefully extracted the wonderful stones, washed them and put
them back in the bag. "Come," said the travellers, "Join us in a
meal." At this a quantity of cooked rice and lentils was made
available by the villagers and all who partook of the curry
pronounced it the best they had ever tasted. It is said that Stone
Curry is still made in the area . . .'

Vegetables

Where the recipes include a variety of vegetables, once the basic techniques have been mastered, it is worth experimenting with other vegetables, especially the unfamiliar ones which can sometimes be bought in Asian stores according to season. In this way many other flavour choices become available as well as improving your experience of how certain vegetables behave in combination.

Curries

Pea Curry (*Matar ki kari*)

2 tablespoons ghee
1 onion, chopped

1 tablespoon chopped
   coriander leaf

1 inch (2·5 cm) piece ginger,
   finely chopped
1 teaspoon turmeric powder
½ teaspoon cumin powder
1 teaspoon coriander powder
½ teaspoon paprika or chilli
   powder

2 cups peas
1 teaspoon salt
1 teaspoon garam masala
1 tablespoon lemon juice

Heat ghee and fry the onion, coriander leaf and ginger till golden. Add the spices and fry for a few minutes. Stir in the peas and salt, mix well, cover and cook gently till the peas are tender. Before serving sprinkle with garam masala and lemon juice. Serve with rice. Tomatoes go well with this recipe. Add them with the peas. Broad beans and other green beans can be prepared in this way.

Peas and Potatoes (*Matar ālū*)

Use the same recipe as above, adding 1 lb (450 g) half-cooked chopped potatoes with the peas and an extra teaspoon of salt. The spices may be slightly increased in quantity according to taste.

Mushroom Curry (*Khumbi ki kari*)

1 lb (450 g) mushrooms,
   chopped
1 lb (450 g) potatoes, chopped
2 tablespoons ghee
2 onions, sliced
1 inch (2·5 cm) piece ginger,
   finely chopped
1 tablespoon chopped
   coriander leaves

1 teaspoon turmeric powder
½ teaspoon paprika or chilli
   powder
2 teaspoons salt
3 tomatoes, sliced
1 teaspoon garam masala
1 tablespoon lemon juice
   (optional)

Wash the mushrooms and potatoes before cutting. Heat ghee and fry the onion, ginger and coriander leaf till the onion begins to turn golden. Add turmeric, paprika and salt and fry for two minutes. Add the mushrooms, potatoes and tomatoes and cook gently till the potatoes are tender. Stir in garam masala and lemon juice just before serving. Serve with dal and rice.

Beans, turnips and many other vegetables can be prepared using the above recipes.

Cauliflower Curry (*Phūlgobi ki kari*)

1 cauliflower (1½–2 lbs/ 675–900 g)
4 cloves garlic
1 inch (2·5 cm) piece ginger
1 teaspoon salt
½ teaspoon paprika or chilli powder

1 teaspoon turmeric powder
juice of ½ lemon
2 tablespoons ghee
1 teaspoon garam masala

Wash the cauliflower and cut into sprigs. Grind the garlic, ginger, salt, paprika and turmeric, adding the lemon juice to make a paste. Heat ghee and fry the paste for a few minutes. Add the cauliflower, cover and cook on a low heat. When nearly done sprinkle over the garam masala.

This recipe can be used for steamed masala cauliflower, see under Dams.

Aubergine Curry (*Baingan ki kari*)

1½ lbs (675 g) aubergines
2 tablespoons ghee
1 teaspoon turmeric powder
4 cloves
1 teaspoon cumin powder
1 teaspoon coriander powder
6 black peppercorns
1 inch (2·5 cm) piece ginger, finely chopped

½ teaspoon paprika or chilli powder
2 tablespoons chopped coriander leaves
3 tomatoes, chopped
1 teaspoon salt
juice of ½ lemon

Cut aubergines into cubes and soak in cold water. Heat ghee and fry the spices for two minutes. Add the tomatoes, salt and aubergines. Stir for five minutes, add the lemon juice, cover and cook slowly. Add a little water to prevent sticking. Serve hot with rice.

Banana Curry (*Kela ki kari*)

4 cloves garlic
1 teaspoon salt
½ teaspoon paprika or chilli
   powder
2 teaspoons coriander seeds
½ teaspoon turmeric powder

3 tablespoons ghee
2 onions, chopped
6 bananas, sliced
2 tablespoons yogurt
1 teaspoon garam masala

Grind the garlic, salt, paprika, coriander and turmeric to a paste. Heat ghee and fry the onions till golden. Stir in the masala paste and fry for a few minutes. Add the bananas and brown. Stir in the yogurt and garam masala and cook till the bananas are soft, adding a little hot water if necessary. Serve hot garnished with chopped coriander leaves.

Yam Curry (*Arbi ki kari*)

1½ lbs (675 g) yam
ghee for frying
2 onions, chopped
1 inch (2·5 cm) piece ginger,
   finely chopped
2 green chillies, chopped
   (optional)

1 teaspoon salt
½ teaspoon paprika or chilli
   powder
1½ teaspoons coriander powder
½ teaspoon garam masala

Wash, peel and soak the yam in salted water for half an hour. Drain and cut into cubes. Deep fry till tender and drain. In a separate pan fry the onions in 2 tablespoons of ghee, add the spices and fry for a few minutes. Stir in the yam and fry gently for five minutes. Garnish with chopped coriander leaves and serve hot with rice.

Peanut Curry (*Phali ki kari*)

2 onions, chopped
2 tablespoons ghee
1 cup grated coconut
1 teaspoon poppy seeds

1 teaspoon coriander seeds
½ teaspoon turmeric powder
½ teaspoon paprika or chilli
   powder

½ lb (225 g) peanuts
2 tomatoes, chopped
1 teaspoon soft brown sugar

1 teaspoon salt
coriander leaves

Fry the onions in ghee till golden. Grind the coconut with poppy seeds, coriander, turmeric and paprika to make a paste. Add the paste to the fried onions and fry for a few minutes. Stir in the nuts, tomatoes, sugar and salt. Fry for a further two minutes and add a cup of hot water. Cook gently till the nuts are tender. Garnish with chopped coriander leaves and serve hot with puris.

Gujerati Vegetable Curry

2 tablespoons ghee
1 lb (450 g) par-cooked potatoes, cubed
1 lb (450 g) peas
½ lb (225 g) French beans, sliced
1 onion, chopped

½ teaspoon cumin powder
1 teaspoon coriander powder
1 teaspoon turmeric powder
1 teaspoon paprika or chilli powder
2 teaspoons salt
1 teaspoon soft brown sugar

Heat ghee and fry the potatoes, peas and beans. Remove and lightly fry the onion. Add all spices and fry for a few minutes. Add the vegetables, salt, sugar and half a cup of hot water. Cover and simmer till all the vegetables are cooked.

Bengali Vegetable Curry

4 tablespoons ghee
½ teaspoon mustard seeds
½ teaspoon fenugreek seeds
½ teaspoon fennel or aniseed
1 teaspoon cumin powder
½ teaspoon paprika or chilli powder

1 bay leaf, broken
1 lb (450 g) potatoes, cubed
1 aubergine, cubed
1 cup cubed marrow or pumpkin
1 cup peas
1½ teaspoons salt
1 teaspoon soft brown sugar

Heat ghee and fry the mustard seeds, fenugreek, fennel, cumin, paprika and bay leaf. When the mustard seeds sputter, add the potatoes and fry for a few minutes then add the rest of the vegetables. Stir fry for five minutes. Sprinkle with salt and sugar and enough water to cook the vegetables. Cover and simmer till tender.

Nepali Vegetable Curry

4 tablespoons ghee
2 onions, chopped
1 bay leaf, broken
½ teaspoon black pepper
4 green chillies, chopped
6 cloves garlic, finely chopped
1½ inch (4 cm) piece ginger, finely chopped
½ teaspoon turmeric powder
2 teaspoons salt

2 lbs (1 kilo) potatoes or other vegetables, cubed
1 cauliflower, split into florets
6 spring onions, chopped
2 cups peas
6 tomatoes, quartered
1 tablespoon coriander leaves, chopped
2 teaspoons coriander seeds
1 tablespoon cumin seeds

Heat ghee and fry the onion till golden. Add bay leaf, pepper, chillies, garlic, ginger, turmeric and salt. Stir in the potatoes and fry till browned. Add remaining ingredients and a cup of hot water. Cook gently till all the vegetables are tender. Any other vegetables may be added to or substituted for the list of ingredients.

Dams

Damming is a form of delicate steaming where the vegetables retain their form. They should never be reduced to a pulp.

Spiked Steamed Potatoes (*Ālu dam*)

2 lbs (1 kilo) small potatoes
1 onion, chopped
4 cloves garlic
1 inch (2·5 cm) piece ginger
½ teaspoon paprika or chilli powder
juice of 1 lemon

1 teaspoon salt
3 cups milk
1 inch (2·5 cm) piece cinnamon, broken
4 green cardamoms
6 cloves
4 tablespoons ghee

Peel the potatoes and prick all over with a fork till they become spongy. Leave to soak in water. Meanwhile, grind the onion, garlic, ginger, turmeric and paprika to a paste. Mix the paste with lemon juice, salt and milk, stir well and pour over the drained potatoes. Heat ghee and fry the cinnamon, cardamoms and cloves. Add the potato mixture, cover and simmer till the potatoes are cooked. Serve hot like a curry.

A similar technique can be used where the potatoes are first parboiled and smothered with a yogurt paste:

2 lbs (1 kilo) potatoes
1 cup yogurt
1 teaspoon turmeric powder
1 teaspoon garam masala
1 teaspoon salt
2 tablespoons ghee

3 bay leaves, broken
½ teaspoon paprika or chilli powder
½ teaspoon brown sugar
2 tablespoons chopped coriander leaves

Boil the potatoes until half cooked, peel and prick all over with a fork. Beat into the yogurt the turmeric, garam masala and salt until the yogurt is smooth. Heat ghee and fry the bay leaves and paprika for two minutes. Add the sugar and stir till it begins to brown. Stir into the yogurt. Cover the potatoes with this yogurt paste and

74

sprinkle with chopped coriander leaf. Cover and bake in a moderate oven till the potatoes are tender and encrusted with the paste (15–25 minutes). Serve hot.

Kashmiri Spiked Potatoes (*Kashmiri ālū dam*)

1 lb (450 g) potatoes
ghee for frying
1½ cups water
½ teaspoon paprika or chilli
   powder
1 teaspoon coriander powder

½ teaspoon Kashmiri garam
   masala
½ teaspoon salt
1 inch (2·5 cm) piece ginger,
   finely chopped

Boil the potatoes until half cooked, peel and prick all over with a fork. Fry in ghee till golden. Remove and drain. Bring the water to the boil with paprika, coriander, Kashmiri garam masala, salt and ginger. Add the potatoes, cover and simmer gently till tender. Garnish with chopped coriander leaf and serve hot with leavened puris (khamiri puri, see recipe).

Steamed Green Beans (*Phali dam*)

1 teaspoon ghee
12 oz (340 g) French or string
   beans, sliced
1 onion, sliced

½ inch (15 mm) piece ginger,
   finely chopped
½ teaspoon salt
½ teaspoon fennel seeds

Boil half a cup of water with ghee. Add the beans, onion and seasoning. Mix well, cover and steam for a few minutes till the beans are tender but firm. If any moisture is left this should be driven off by raising the heat. Serve hot.

Steamed Masala Cauliflower (*Phūlgobi dam*)

For the cauliflower:

1 cauliflower, cut into
   sprigs
6 cloves garlic

1 inch (2·5 cm) piece ginger
½ teaspoon paprika or chilli
   powder

1 teaspoon turmeric powder

½ teaspoon garam masala

1 teaspoon salt

juice of ½ lemon

Wash the cauliflower, cut in sprigs and place in a pan with 1½ cups water. Grind the rest of the ingredients, adding lemon juice to make a paste. Spread over the cauliflower. Bring the water to the boil, cover and steam till tender (about 10–15 minutes). This steamed cauliflower may be enriched by smothering with a curd masala paste, five minutes before the end:

1 tablespoon ghee

1 onion, finely chopped

4 cloves garlic, finely chopped

1 inch (2·5 cm) piece ginger

1 teaspoon coriander seeds

½ teaspoon cumin seeds

6 cloves

8 black peppercorns

1 inch (2·5 cm) piece cinnamon, broken

4 green cardamoms, skinned

10 almonds, blanched

2 tomatoes, chopped

1 teaspoon salt

1 cup yogurt

Heat ghee and lightly fry the onion and garlic. Grind the ginger, spices and almonds. Add to the fried onions with tomatoes and salt. Fry for a few minutes, slowly stirring in the yogurt. Pour over the cauliflower, cover and continue simmering till tender.

This recipe can be used with other green vegetables or a mixture of them. Take care not to overcook.

Steamed Vegetables (*Sabzi dam*)

1 teaspoon turmeric powder

2 tablespoons mint leaves

¼ inch (15 mm) piece ginger

4 cloves garlic

juice of 1 lemon

1 cup yogurt

½ lb (225 g) courgettes, chopped

½ lb (225 g) marrow or pumpkin, peeled and cubed

½ lb (225 g) white cabbage or cauliflower, chopped

½ lb (225 g) mushrooms, sliced

1 tablespoon ghee

1 onion, finely chopped

Grind the turmeric, mint, ginger and garlic with lemon juice. Add yogurt to this paste and mix well. Cover the vegetables with the yogurt paste and leave to soak. Heat ghee and lightly fry the onion. Add a cup of hot water or vegetable stock. Put in the vegetables and yogurt paste, cover well and simmer till tender. Add extra water or stock if necessary to prevent sticking. Serve hot.

This recipe uses soft vegetables. Firmer vegetables may be substituted and cooking time will vary accordingly.

Foogaths

Foogaths are vegetables fried with onions and a little masala. The following recipes are from Maharashtra.

Cabbage Foogath (*Gobi fūgath*)

4 tablespoons ghee
2 onions, finely chopped
2 cloves garlic, finely chopped
1 inch (2·5 cm) piece ginger,
    finely chopped

½ teaspoon paprika or chilli
    powder
1 cabbage, shredded
1 teaspoon salt
½ coconut, grated

Heat ghee and lightly fry the onion, ginger and paprika. Add the washed and shredded cabbage, sprinkle with salt and stir-fry. When nearly cooked, stir in the coconut and continue frying till tender.

Radishes, beans and other firm vegetables may be cooked this way.

Pumpkin or Marrow Foogath (*Kadū fūgath*)

3 tablespoons ghee
1 onion, sliced
½ teaspoon turmeric powder
½ inch (15 mm) piece ginger
2 cloves garlic
½ teaspoon paprika or chilli
    powder

1 lb (450 g) pumpkin or marrow,
    peeled and cubed
juice of ½ lemon
½ teaspoon salt

Heat ghee and lightly fry the onion. Grind the turmeric, ginger, garlic and paprika to form a paste. Stir this into the fried onion with the pumpkin pieces, lemon juice and salt. Add a little water and cook on a medium heat till tender.

Lady Finger Foogath (*Bhindi fūgath*)

2 tablespoons ghee
1 onion, chopped
12 Lady fingers (okras),
    washed and sliced
1 tablespoon grated coconut

2 green chillies, chopped
    (optional)
½ inch (15 mm) piece ginger
2 cloves garlic
½ teaspoon salt

Heat ghee and fry the onion with the bhindis. Grind the coconut, chillies, ginger, garlic and salt and stir into the bhindis. Stir-fry gently till tender.

Plantain Foogath (*Kela fūgath*)

6 plantains or green bananas
½ inch (15 mm) piece ginger
4 cloves garlic
½ teaspoon turmeric powder
½ teaspoon cumin seeds
½ teaspoon paprika or chilli
    powder

4 tablespoons ghee
1 onion, sliced
½ teaspoon salt
½ coconut, grated

Peel the plantains, slice and leave to soak in water for an hour. Grind the ginger, garlic, turmeric, cumin and paprika to a paste. Heat ghee and lightly fry the onion. Add the masala paste and fry for a few minutes. Add the drained plantain slices and salt and stir-fry. When half cooked, stir in the grated coconut and cook till the plantains are tender.

Vegetable Balls *(Koftas)*

Potato Balls *(Ālū kofta)*

1 lb (450 g) potatoes
½ teaspoon salt
4 spring onions, finely chopped
1 cup cooked cauliflower
   florets or peas

1 tablespoon chopped **coriander**
   leaves
1 teaspoon garam masala
juice of ½ lemon
ghee for frying

Cook potatoes in salted water till soft. Peel and mash. Mix in the rest of the ingredients. Divide the mixture into 30–35 small balls. Roll in a little besan (gram flour) or plain flour. Fry in hot ghee till golden. Serve hot for lunch or as a savoury snack. They go well with a cold salad.

Potato Ball Curry Sauce

2 tablespoons ghee
1 onion, finely chopped
2 cloves garlic, finely chopped
½ inch (15 mm) piece ginger,
   finely chopped

1 teaspoon turmeric powder
2 teaspoons coriander powder
½ teaspoon garam masala
4 tomatoes, chopped
1 cup water

Drain the koftas made in the above recipe and keep warm while you prepare the curry sauce. Heat ghee and lightly fry the onion, garlic and ginger. Add the spices and fry for two minutes. Stir in the tomatoes and cook till a thick gravy is formed, adding a cup of water. Serve the hot koftas and pour over the curry sauce. If the koftas are kept in the sauce they tend to absorb the moisture and become soggy.

Pea Balls (*Matar kofta*)

1 lb (450 g) cooked green
  peas
½ lb (225 g) potatoes, boiled
1 teaspoon poppy seeds

½ teaspoon paprika or chilli
  powder
1 tablespoon lemon juice
gram flour (besan)

Mash the ingredients together. Form into balls, rolling in a little besan to bind. Deep-fry in ghee. Serve in the same way as **potato koftas**.

Spinach Balls (*Sāg kofta*)

1½ lbs (675 g) spinach
½ inch (15 mm) piece ginger,
  finely chopped
1 green chilli, chopped
  (optional)

4 cloves garlic, finely chopped
½ teaspoon salt
½ teaspoon garam masala
gram flour (besan)

Wash the spinach and cook for a few minutes in the minimum of water. Purée the spinach in a pestle and mortar or liquidiser. Add the ginger, chilli, garlic, salt, garam masala and enough besan to make a stiff mixture. Roll up into balls and deep-fry. Serve hot with a curry sauce.

Green Banana Balls (*Kela kofta*)

6 green bananas
1 tablespoon ghee
1 onion, finely chopped
2 cloves garlic, finely chopped
½ inch (15 mm) piece ginger,
  finely chopped
1 teaspoon salt

1 teaspoon paprika or chilli
  powder
2 green cardamoms, skinned
  and crushed
½ teaspoon garam masala
1 tablespoon chopped
  coriander leaves

For the filling:

1 small onion, finely chopped
1 tablespoon ghee
20 almonds, blanched and
  chopped

20 pistachios, chopped
1 heaped tablespoon sultanas
1 dessertspoon coriander
  leaves, finely chopped

Boil the bananas in salted water till soft. Peel and mash. Heat ghee and fry the onion, garlic and ginger. Stir in the mashed banana, salt, paprika, cardamom, garam masala and coriander leaves. Stir-fry for two minutes. When cool mix in a few spoons of milk to make a dough-like mixture. Shape into balls with the help of a little flour. Make a filling by frying the onion in ghee with the rest of the ingredients. Put a teaspoon of filling in each ball and roll up again. Keep warm and serve with a curry sauce. Garnish with chopped coriander leaves.

Marrow Balls (*Gūda kofta*)

1 lb (450 g) marrow
2 green chillies, finely
  chopped
1 onion, finely chopped

2 tablespoons gram flour
  (besan)
$\frac{1}{2}$ teaspoon salt
ghee for frying

Peel the marrow and chop. Boil in minimum water till soft. Mix in the rest of the ingredients and form into small balls with the help of some dry flour. Deep-fry in ghee. Serve hot with sauce, garnished with coriander leaves.

Tarkaris

Tarkari is a technique where the vegetables are fried in ghee and their own juice. The heat is raised towards the end of the cooking to impregnate the taste and aroma of the spices.

Potato, Tomato and Onion Tarkari (*Ālū tamātar pīāz tarkari*)

2 tablespoons ghee
2 onions, chopped
1 lb (450 g) potatoes, par-cooked
2 teaspoons salt
  1 inch (2·5 cm) piece ginger, finely chopped
  1 teaspoon soft brown sugar

½ teaspoon paprika or chilli powder
½ teaspoon turmeric powder
1 lb (450 g) tomatoes, chopped
2 green chillies, sliced (optional)
½ teaspoon garam masala
chopped coriander leaves

Heat ghee and gently fry the onion with the chopped potatoes, salt, paprika and turmeric in a covered pan. When nearly cooked add the tomato, chillies, ginger and sugar. Raise the heat, shake to prevent sticking, and cook till the potatoes are ready. Serve sprinkled with garam masala and coriander leaves.

Green Pepper and Tomato Tarkari (*Simla mirch tamātar tarkari*)

3 tablespoons ghee
8 oz (225 g) green peppers (capsicum), sliced
1 inch (2·5 cm) piece ginger, finely chopped
1½ teaspoons salt

pinch black pepper
1 lb (450 g) tomatoes, chopped
2 teaspoons soft brown sugar
chopped coriander leaves
½ teaspoon garam masala

Heat ghee and fry green pepper, ginger, 1 teaspoon of salt and a pinch of pepper for a few minutes. Add the tomato, ½ teaspoon salt and sugar. Raise the heat and stir-fry for five minutes. Serve garnished with coriander leaves and garam masala.

Aubergine and Green Pepper Tarkari (*Baingan simla mirch tarkari*)

3 tablespoons ghee
2 onions, chopped
12 oz (340 g) aubergines, sliced
12 oz (340 g) green peppers (capsicum), sliced
2 teaspoons salt

½ teaspoon paprika or chilli powder
2 tomatoes, chopped
½ teaspoon garam masala
chopped coriander leaves

Heat ghee and fry onion. Add the aubergine and capsicum slices. Stir-fry with salt and paprika till nearly cooked. Add tomatoes, raise the heat and cook till tender. Sprinkle with garam masala and coriander leaves.

Masala Cabbage (*Band gobi tarkari*)

1½ lb (675 g) cabbage
2 tablespoons ghee
1 onion, finely sliced
1 inch (2·5 cm) piece ginger, finely chopped
1 teaspoon turmeric powder

1 teaspoon salt
½ teaspoon paprika or chilli powder
1 teaspoon garam masala
juice of ½ lemon
pinch of mace

Wash the cabbage and shred. A firm white cabbage gives the best results. Heat ghee and fry the onion and garlic. Add the turmeric, salt and paprika. Stir-fry for a few minutes then cover and cook on a medium heat till tender. Uncover and dry off any remaining water by raising the heat. Sprinkle with garam masala, lemon juice and mace.

Bhartas

To make a bharta, the vegetable is cooked to purée consistency, drying off the excess moisture.

Cauliflower Purée (*Phūlgobi bharta*)

1 cauliflower
3 tablespoons ghee
2 onions, finely chopped
2 teaspoons mustard seeds
4 cloves garlic
½ inch (15 mm) piece ginger
1 teaspoon turmeric powder

2 teaspoons coriander seeds
1 teaspoon cumin seeds
½ teaspoon black peppercorns
½ teaspoon paprika
2 tablespoons yogurt
1 teaspoon salt

Wash and slice the cauliflower. Heat ghee and fry the onion, cauliflower and mustard seeds till golden. Grind the slices to a paste and add to the cauliflower. Fry for two minutes and stir in the yogurt. Add 2 cups of water or milk and simmer till the cauliflower is soft and the excess moisture has been driven off.

Carrot and Radish Purée (*Gājar mūli bharta*)

½ lb (225 g) carrots
½ lb (225 g) radishes
2 tablespoons ghee
½ inch (15 mm) piece ginger, finely chopped
1 onion, finely chopped

1 teaspoon salt
½ teaspoon garam masala
½ teaspoon paprika or chilli powder
2 tomatoes, chopped

Clean and trim the carrots and radishes. Chop and boil in minimum water till soft and mash. Heat ghee and fry ginger and onion. Add the mashed vegetables, salt, garam masala, paprika and tomatoes. Mix well and cook till nearly all the juice is gone.

Tomato Purée (*Tamātar bharta*)

1 lb (450 g) tomatoes
1 tablespoon ghee
½ onion, finely chopped
2 bay leaves
1 tablespoon mint leaves,
  chopped

pinch of black pepper
½ teaspoon salt
1 cup yogurt or cream

Peeled tinned tomatoes are ideal for this purpose. Mash well or chop and sieve fresh tomatoes. Heat ghee and fry the onion and spices. Stir in the tomato and yogurt. Simmer till the excess moisture is driven off.

Aubergine Purée (*Baingan bharta*)

This is a popular bharta in the Punjab.

1 lb (450 g) aubergines
3 tablespoons ghee
1 onion, finely chopped
2 tomatoes, chopped
1 dessertspoon chopped
  coriander leaves
1 teaspoon coriander powder

½ teaspoon paprika or chilli
  powder
½ teaspoon turmeric powder
½ teaspoon cumin powder
1 teaspoon fennel seeds ground
1 teaspoon salt

Heat the aubergines till the skin blackens and the flesh becomes soft. Peel and mash. Heat ghee and lightly fry the onion, tomatoes, and coriander leaves. Add the spices and salt and stir-fry for two minutes. Add the aubergine pulp and cook on a low heat for five more minutes. Serve with chapatis or as a curry side dish.

Turnip Purée (*Shalgam bharta*)

1 lb (450 g) turnips
2 tablespoons ghee
½ inch (15 mm) piece ginger,
  finely chopped
1 onion, finely chopped

2 teaspoons ground aniseed
  or fennel
1 teaspoon ground fenugreek seeds
½ teaspoon fresh ground
  black pepper

$\frac{1}{2}$ teaspoon paprika or chilli
    powder
$\frac{1}{2}$ teaspoon garam masala

1 teaspoon salt
1 teaspoon soft brown sugar

Peel the turnips and cut in small pieces. Boil in minimum water till soft. Mash. Heat ghee and fry the ginger and onion. Add the spices, mashed turnip, salt and sugar. Mix well and cook gently till the excess moisture has been driven off.

Parsnips and swedes may be prepared using this recipe.

Potato Purée (*Ālū bharta*)

1 lb (450 g) potatoes
1 teaspoon salt
1 tablespoon ghee
1 onion, chopped

1 green chilli, chopped
1 tablespoon chopped
    coriander leaves

Boil the potatoes in salted water. Mash. Heat ghee and fry the rest of the ingredients till the onion turns golden. Add the potatoes and mix well.

Spinach Purée (*Sāg bharta*)

1 lb (450 g) spinach or mixed
    greens
1 turnip, swede or parsnip
1 teaspoon salt
1 tablespoon ghee

1 onion, finely chopped
$\frac{1}{2}$ inch (15 mm) piece ginger,
    finely chopped
$\frac{1}{2}$ teaspoon paprika or chilli
    powder

Wash the greens and turnip and cut fine. Boil in a covered pan with a cup of water and salt. When tender, remove from the heat and mash. Heat ghee and lightly fry the onion, ginger and paprika for two minutes. Add the mashed greens and stir-fry till the excess moisture has been driven off.

Stuffed Vegetables

Stuffed Cabbage Rolls

4 tablespoons gram flour (besan)
6–10 large cabbage leaves
½ teaspoon salt
1 onion, finely chopped
2 cloves garlic, finely chopped
1 tablespoon ghee and ghee for frying
8 oz (225 g) mashed potato
½ inch (15 mm) piece ginger, finely chopped

2 green chillies, chopped (optional)
1 tablespoon chopped coriander leaves
½ teaspoon salt
¼ teaspoon paprika or chilli powder
½ teaspoon garam masala

Make a batter with besan flour, a pinch of salt and pepper and half a cup of water. Mix well and leave to stand. Boil the cabbage leaves rapidly in salted water. Remove and drain. Prepare the filling by lightly frying the onion and garlic in ghee. Add mashed potato and the rest of the ingredients. Stir-fry for five minutes. Divide the filling and put a portion on each cabbage leaf, folding in the edges and rolling up. Dip the rolls in the batter and fry in ghee. Serve hot.

An alternative to frying in batter is to sprinkle with lemon juice, a pinch of salt and pepper, roll in dry flour and gently fry in ghee. Serve the rolls in a sauce made from fried onions, ginger and tomato purée. Fry these ingredients and stir in water till the required consistency is obtained. Sprinkle with chopped fried cashew nuts.

Stuffed Green Peppers

6 medium-sized green peppers (capsicum)
4 tablespoons ghee
1 teaspoon coriander powder
½ teaspoon garam masala
½ teaspoon paprika or chilli powder
¼ teaspoon turmeric powder
½ inch (15 mm) piece ginger, finely chopped
½ lb (225 g) mixed vegetables, chopped
1 potato, peeled and diced
juice of 1 lemon
2 teaspoons salt

Wash the peppers and cut a thin slice from the top of each pepper. Core and remove the seeds. Heat 2 tablespoons ghee and fry the spices for two minutes. Add the vegetables and potato, lemon juice and salt. Cook till the vegetables are tender. Stuff the peppers with the mixture, close with the sliced tops and gently fry in the rest of the ghee for five minutes. Add a cup of water, cover and simmer till the peppers are tender.

Stuffed Marrow

2 small marrows

For the stuffing:

1 tablespoon ghee
1 onion, finely chopped
2 green chillies, sliced (optional)
1 tablespoon chopped coriander leaves
1 cup green peas
1 cup panir cubes
1 teaspoon salt

For the sauce:

2 tablespoons ghee
2 onions, chopped
1 teaspoon salt
1 inch (2·5 cm) piece ginger
1 teaspoon coriander seeds
½ teaspoon turmeric powder
¼ teaspoon cumin seeds
1 teaspoon garam masala
½ teaspoon paprika or chilli powder

Peel and trim the marrows. Cut off the tops to use as lids. Scoop out the seeds and a little flesh to make a hollow. Put any surplus flesh in the stuffing. Half cook the marrows by boiling in salted water. Remove and drain. Prepare the stuffing by lightly frying the onion till golden. Add the chillies, coriander leaves, peas, panir and salt. Stir-fry for a few minutes. Stuff the marrows and put on the lids. Heat ghee for the sauce and fry the onion. Grind the rest of the ingredients, adding a little water to form a paste. Add to the onions and fry for a few minutes. Pour in enough hot water to make a thick gravy. Put in the stuffed marrows, cover and simmer till tender.

Stuffed Tomatoes

In this recipe from Gujerat, the tomatoes are stuffed with rice. A stuffing of mixed vegetables could be used as in the next recipe.

6 large tomatoes
2 tablespoons ghee
1 onion, finely chopped
½ teaspoon turmeric powder

½ teaspoon garam masala
½ teaspoon salt
1 cup boiled rice

Wash the tomatoes and cut off the tops. Scoop out the seed pulp and keep aside. Lightly fry the onions till golden. Add the seed pulp and the rest of the ingredients and fry for a few minutes. Leave to cool and stuff the tomatoes with the mixture. Put on the lids and bake in a moderate oven for ten minutes.

Stuffed Tomato and Potato

6 large tomatoes
1 tablespoon ghee
1 small onion, finely chopped
2 cloves garlic, finely chopped
1 inch (2·5 cm) piece ginger, finely chopped
½ teaspoon paprika or chilli powder

½ teaspoon garam masala
1 teaspoon salt
½ cup green peas
2 carrots, diced
½ cup panir cubes

For the potato cases:

1 lb (450 g) potatoes
2 tablespoons gram flour (besan)

½ teaspoon salt
½ teaspoon garam masala

Wash the tomatoes and slice off the tops. Scoop out the pulp and keep aside. To make the stuffing, fry the onion, garlic and ginger. Stir in the spices and fry for two minutes. Add the vegetables and panir. Fill the tomatoes with the cooked mixture and cover with the tops. Put the potatoes on to boil and prepare a thick batter with besan flour, water, salt and garam masala. Mix well and leave to stand. Mash the potatoes with a little melted ghee. Cover each stuffed tomato with potato. Beat the batter again and pour some over each potato-covered tomato. Fry in ghee till golden. The tomatoes may be eaten at each of the three stages by baking in a moderate oven or frying in ghee.

Potato Dishes

Potato and Greens (*Ālū sāg*)

2 tablespoons ghee
1 onion, finely chopped
2 cloves garlic, finely chopped
1 inch (2·5 cm) piece ginger,
    finely chopped
1 teaspoon turmeric powder
1 teaspoon salt

½ teaspoon paprika or chilli
    powder
1 teaspoon coriander powder
1 lb (450 g) potatoes
1 lb (450 g) spinach or greens
1 teaspoon garam masala

Heat ghee and lightly fry the onion, garlic and ginger. Add the salt and spices and fry for two minutes. While the spices are frying wash the potatoes and chop. Add to the spices and fry till half cooked. Meanwhile wash the spinach and chop finely. Stir into the potatoes and continue frying till tender. Sprinkle with garam masala before serving.

Potato and Green Bananas (*Patiya*)

1 lb (450 g) potatoes, cubed
½ lb (225 g) green bananas,
    peeled and sliced
1 teaspoon salt
1 teaspoon black pepper
1 teaspoon turmeric powder

2 cups water
1 fresh coconut, grated
1 tablespoon ghee
a few curry leaves
2 teaspoons mustard seeds

Put the potatoes and bananas in a pan and sprinkle with salt, pepper and turmeric. Cover with water and boil till tender, adding extra water if necessary. When the potatoes are nearly done add the grated coconut and cook for a further ten minutes. Heat ghee and fry the curry leaves and mustard seeds. When the seeds begin to jump, stir into the patiya. Serve with a curry or rice and tomato chutney. Patiyas come from South India.

Fried Masala Potatoes

1½ lbs (675 g) potatoes, chopped
ghee for deep-frying
1 teaspoon poppy seeds
10 almonds
1 teaspoon cumin seeds
1 tablespoon coriander seeds
6 cloves
10 black peppercorns
5 green cardamoms

1 inch (2·5 cm) piece ginger
4 cloves garlic
2 onions, finely chopped
1 teaspoon paprika or chilli
  powder
½ teaspoon turmeric powder
2 teaspoons salt
2 cups yogurt
½ teaspoon garam masala

Prick the potatoes all over with a fork and leave to soak in water for half an hour. Drain and dry. Deep-fry in ghee till golden. Remove and drain. Meanwhile, grind the poppy seeds, almonds, cumin, coriander, cloves, peppercorns and cardamoms with the ginger and garlic, adding a little water to make a paste. Fry the onions in two tablespoons ghee, stir in the paprika, turmeric, salt and the masala paste. Fry for five minutes and stir in the yogurt. Add the fried potatoes and garam masala and cook for a further five minutes. Serve hot with puris.

Pea Dishes

Peas and Khoya *(Khoya matar)*

This Kashmiri recipe uses khoya which is made by reducing milk to a thick paste over a gentle heat. It is more convenient to use dried milk as given here.

1 cup dried full-cream milk
3 tablespoons ghee
1 teaspoon coriander powder
1 teaspoon turmeric powder
½ inch (15 mm) piece ginger, finely chopped
1 teaspoon salt
½ teaspoon paprika
1 cup yogurt
1 cup peas
3 tomatoes, chopped
chopped coriander leaves
½ teaspoon Kashmiri garam masala

Mix the dried milk and enough water (about 4 tablespoons) to form an almost dry lump. Fry in ghee till golden. Stir in coriander, turmeric, ginger, salt and paprika and fry for two minutes. Add yogurt, peas and tomatoes. Cook for five minutes or till the peas are tender. Sprinkle with coriander leaves and Kashmiri garam masala. Serve with plain rice.

Peas and Carrots *(matar gājar)*

1 onion, finely sliced
2 tablespoons chopped coriander leaves
2 tablespoons ghee
1 teaspoon turmeric powder
1 teaspoon garam masala
1 teaspoon salt
½ teaspoon paprika or chilli powder
½ lb (225 g) young carrots, chopped
1½ cups green peas
1 tablespoon lemon juice

94

Lightly fry the onions and coriander in ghee. Add turmeric, garam masala, salt and paprika and fry for two minutes. Add the carrots and peas. Mix well and cook on a low heat till tender. Stir in lemon juice before serving. Serve hot with curry and rice.

Peas and Panir (*Matar panir*)

2 cups panir cubes
4 tablespoons ghee
1 inch (2·5 cm) piece ginger
1 teaspoon turmeric powder
½ teaspoon paprika or chilli powder
1 teaspoon cumin seeds
2 green cardamoms, skinned
1 inch (2·5 cm) piece cinnamon, broken

2 onions, finely chopped
1 teaspoon mustard seeds
1 teaspoon poppy seeds
1½ teaspoons salt
2 cups peas
4 tomatoes, chopped
2 cups water
1 teaspoon garam masala
1 tablespoon lemon juice

Fry the panir cubes in ghee till golden. Remove and drain. Grind the ginger, turmeric, paprika, cumin, cardamoms and cinnamon, adding a little water to form a paste. Fry the onions, mustard seeds and poppy seeds till golden. Add the paste and salt and fry for two minutes. Add the peas and tomatoes, stir-fry for a few minutes, add water, cover and cook till the peas are tender. Before serving sprinkle with garam masala and lemon juice. Serve hot with rice or chapatis.

Aubergine Dishes

Aubergine and Tomato *(Baingan tamātar)*

1 lb (450 g) aubergines, chopped
2 tablespoons ghee
1 onion, sliced
½ teaspoon paprika or chilli powder

1 lb (450 g) tomatoes, sliced
1 teaspoon salt
½ teaspoon garam masala

Soak the aubergines in salted water. Fry the onion in ghee with paprika till golden. Add the drained aubergines, cover and cook till nearly tender. Add the tomatoes, salt and garam masala. Cover and continue cooking till the aubergines are ready.

Aubergine Moli *(Baingan moli)*

Molis are made in South and West India, the Goan molis tasting more sour.

2 aubergines
1 teaspoon turmeric powder
1 teaspoon salt
4 tablespoons ghee
1 teaspoon cumin seeds
1 onion, sliced

2 cloves garlic, finely chopped
½ teaspoon paprika or chilli
powder
1 inch (2·5 cm) piece ginger,
finely chopped
1 cup thick coconut milk

Slice the aubergines and dip in a thick batter made from turmeric, salt and water. Cover all sides and leave to soak. Heat ghee and fry the cumin seeds. Add the aubergine slices and fry till golden. Remove. Fry the onion, garlic, paprika and ginger till golden. Add the coconut milk, bring to the boil and add the fried aubergines. Simmer till the sauce thickens and serve with rice.

Lady Finger Dishes

Lady Fingers (*Bhindi*)

1 lb (450 g) Lady Fingers (okras)
6 tablespoons ghee
2 onions, finely chopped
4 cloves garlic, finely chopped
1 teaspoon salt
½ teaspoon turmeric powder
1 teaspoon garam masala
½ teaspoon paprika or chilli powder
1 cup yogurt
chopped coriander leaves

Trim the washed bhindis and fry in ghee till golden. Remove. Fry the onion and garlic till the onion begins to brown. Add salt, turmeric, garam masala and paprika. Fry for a few minutes and add the yogurt. When the ghee separates out add a cup of hot water and simmer to make a sauce. Add the fried bhindis and warm thoroughly. Garnish with coriander leaves and serve hot with rice.

Lady Fingers in Curd (*Bhindi pachadi*)

3 tablespoons ghee
2 lbs (900 g) Lady Fingers (okras), finely sliced
4 tablespoons grated coconut
½ teaspoon cumin seeds
2 cloves garlic
2 cups water
1 cup yogurt
1 teaspoon salt
½ teaspoon paprika or chilli powder
½ teaspoon mustard seeds
1 onion, finely sliced
a few curry leaves

Heat 2 tablespoons ghee and fry the bhindis till golden. Grind the coconut, cumin and garlic. Add this paste to the bhindis, 2 cups of hot water, yogurt and salt. Mix well. Heat another tablespoon of ghee and fry the mustard seeds, onion and curry leaves till the onion turns golden. Stir into the pachadi. Serve with sambhar, aviyal (see recipes) and rice. This dish is frequently eaten cold.

Salad Dishes

Vegetable Salad

1 cup green beans, sliced
1 cup peas
1 cup young carrots, sliced
1 cup cucumber, thinly sliced
crisp salad greens
2 cups yogurt

$\frac{1}{2}$ teaspoon cumin powder
$\frac{1}{2}$ teaspoon paprika or chilli
  powder
$\frac{1}{2}$ teaspoon salt
chopped coriander leaves

Chill the vegetables. Arrange the salad greens round the side of a bowl with the rest of the vegetables in the centre. Beat yogurt till smooth with cumin, paprika and salt. Pour over the vegetables. Sprinkle with coriander or mint leaves.

Spiced Onion Salad (*Cachūmbar*)

2 onions, finely chopped
3 tomatoes, chopped
1 small cucumber, chopped
1 green chilli, finely chopped
  (optional)

1 tablespoon chopped
  coriander leaves
1 teaspoon salt
$\frac{1}{2}$ cup light vinegar or yogurt

Mix the vegetables and sprinkle with salt and vinegar. Leave to stand for half an hour before serving.

Aubergine Salad

2 large aubergines
1 onion, finely chopped
1 tablespoon chopped coriander
   leaves

1 green chilli, chopped
1 teaspoon soft brown sugar
1 tablespoon lemon juice
½ teaspoon salt

Grill or bake the aubergines till the skins are blistered and the pulp becomes soft. Skin and mix the pulp with the rest of the ingredients. Serve chilled.

Beetroot Salad

1 lb (450 g) beetroot, cooked
   and sliced
2 tablespoons finely chopped
   onion
juice of 1 lemon

½ teaspoon salt
pinch of black pepper
pinch of paprika or chilli
   powder
½ teaspoon garam masala

Mix the beetroot and onion. Mix lemon juice, salt, pepper and paprika. Pour over the beetroot. Sprinkle with garam masala and serve chilled with yogurt.

Miscellany

Avial

Many dishes with green bananas are served during the ancient Onam festival on the Malabar coast of South India, an occasion for much feasting, singing and dancing. The four-day festival, held during August or September, commemorates the reign of Mahabali. a mythological king who later became worshipped as a god. His spirit is said to return to earth every Onam time. Avial and olan are favourite Onam festival dishes.

1 aubergine, cubed
1 sweet potato or parsnip,
  cubed
2 green bananas, sliced
1 cup green peas
1 cup green beans or sprouts
1 carrot, sliced
1 onion, sliced
1 green pepper, chopped

1 teaspoon turmeric powder
1 teaspoon cumin powder
a few curry leaves
2 cups water
1 teaspoon salt
4 tomatoes, chopped
juice of 1 lemon
½ coconut grated
1 cup yogurt

Combine the washed vegetables with turmeric, cumin and curry leaves. Add water and salt and simmer till the vegetables are nearly tender. Add any soft frozen vegetables last. Add tomato, lemon juice and coconut. Simmer for five minutes. Lower the heat and stir in the yogurt. Serve with sambhar, yogurt and rice. A variety of vegetables such as potatoes, celery, marrow or pumpkin may be used in this dish. In South India green chillies are also included.

Olan

2 green bananas, sliced
½ cup green beans, sliced
½ cup carrots, sliced
½ cup potatoes, chopped
½ cup marrow, pumpkin or
  cucumber, sliced

½ cup green peas
1 teaspoon salt
2 green chillies
1½ cups coconut milk
a few curry leaves

Cook the washed vegetables in minimum water with salt and chillies. If the peas are frozen, add them when all the other vegetables are tender. Add the coconut milk and curry leaves, boil for a few minutes and serve hot with rice.

Green Peppers and Peanuts *(Phali simla mirch)*

1 lb (450 g) green peppers
  (capsicum)
1 cup coconut, grated
2 tablespoons split gram
  (channa dal)
2 teaspoons sesame seeds
lemon juice

3 tablespoons ghee
1½ cups peanuts, crushed
4 tablespoons sultanas
1 teaspoon soft brown sugar
1 teaspoon salt
1 cup hot water

Wash, core and slice the peppers. Grind the coconut, gram dal and sesame seeds with a little lemon juice to form a paste. Heat ghee and fry the capsicums for two minutes. Stir in the masala paste and fry for a further two minutes. Add the peanuts, sultanas, sugar, salt and water. Cover and simmer till the peppers are tender and the sauce is thick.

Fried Greens *(Bhujia)*

Bhujias made by the poor may be simply a few greens or leafy vegetable tops fried in oil with chillies. In this recipe the vegetables are mixed with spices, cooked and finally flavoured by frying in spiced ghee or oil. The ingredients of this final 'tarka' determine the special flavour of this popular dish. Here is an opportunity to invent your own composition.

½ lb (225 g) green beans, sliced
2 potatoes, chopped
½ lb (225 g) spinach or greens, chopped
1 teaspoon salt
1 teaspoon turmeric powder
2 teaspoons coriander powder
1 teaspoon cumin powder
½ teaspoon paprika or chilli powder

½ teaspoon black pepper
2 tablespoons ghee
2 onions, sliced
2 green chillies, chopped (optional)
4 cloves garlic, finely chopped
1 inch (2·5 cm) piece ginger, finely chopped

Boil the washed vegetables briskly in salted water till the potatoes are tender. Drain, sprinkle with the spices, stir and mix well. Heat ghee in a separate pan and lightly fry the rest of the ingredients. When the onions begin to turn golden, stir in the spiced vegetables and fry for five minutes.

Fried Carrots in Curd (*Korma gājar*)

This is an excellent recipe for swedes, parsnips, potatoes or turnips either substituting for or adding to the carrots.

4 tablespoons ghee
1½ lb (675 g) carrots, chopped
1 inch (2·5 cm) piece ginger, finely chopped
4 cloves garlic, finely chopped
2 teaspoons sesame seeds
2 teaspoons poppy seeds
1 teaspoon turmeric powder

1 teaspoon cumin powder
2 teaspoons coriander powder
½ teaspoon paprika or chilli powder
1 teaspoon salt
1 cup yogurt
chopped coriander leaves

Heat ghee and fry the carrots for a few minutes. Add the onions, ginger, garlic, sesame seeds and poppy seeds and fry till golden. Stir in the spices, salt and carrots and fry for two minutes. Add the yogurt and cook till the carrots are tender. Serve hot, garnished with coriander leaves.

Vegetables Mughal Style *(Sabzi mughlai)*

2 lb (1 kilo) mixed vegetables, chopped
1½ cups grated coconut
20 almonds, blanched
2 tablespoons pistachio nuts
2 tablespoons poppy seeds
½ teaspoon paprika or chilli powder
3 tablespoons ghee
2 onions, sliced
6 cloves
6 cardomoms, crushed
2 inches (5 cm) piece cinnamon, broken
1 cup yogurt
juice of ½ lemon

Wash the vegetables and prepare. Grind the coconut with the almonds, pistachios, poppy seeds and paprika with a little water to form a thick paste. Heat ghee and fry the onions. Stir in the paste, vegetables and the rest of the ingredients. Cover and cook till the vegetables are tender, adding water if necessary. Serve hot with rice or chapatis.

Eggs

In the Hindu conception of creation, the universe emerged from the cosmic egg, or egg of Brahman (Brahmanandā).

Many who refrain from eating meat or fish will eat unfertilised eggs. Since these are the most common form of egg which can be purchased, a number of egg recipes are included here.

Egg Curry *(Andā ka kari)*

1 onion, finely chopped
4 tablespoons ghee
2 cloves garlic
1 inch (2·5 cm) piece ginger
½ teaspoon paprika or chilli powder
1 teaspoon coriander seeds

1 teaspoon turmeric powder
½ teaspoon cumin seeds
1 teaspoon salt
4 tomatoes, chopped
2 tablespoons coriander leaves
8 hard-boiled eggs, halved
1 teaspoon garam masala

Lightly fry the onion in ghee. Meanwhile grind the garlic, ginger and spices. Add this masala paste to the onion and fry for two minutes. Stir in the salt, tomatoes and coriander leaves and simmer till the sauce begins to thicken. Add the eggs, sprinkle with garam masala and heat through for five minutes. A tablespoon of lemon juice may be added before serving. Serve hot with rice or a vegetable dish.

Molis are mild curries from Goa. An egg moli can be made using a similar recipe and adding 1 cup coconut milk and a tablespoon of vinegar, lemon juice or tamarind water with the tomatoes.

Egg and Curd Curry (*Korma andā*)

8 hard-boiled eggs, halved
1 teaspoon turmeric powder
1 cup yogurt
2 teaspoons poppy seeds
1 teaspoon sesame seeds
2 tablespoons ground almonds

a few curry leaves
½ teaspoon paprika or chilli powder
1 teaspoon salt
2 tablespoons lemon juice

Cover the eggs in a thin paste made from turmeric and a little water. Heat the yogurt and add the poppy seeds, sesame seeds, almonds, curry leaves, paprika and salt. Cook gently till the sauce thickens. Stir in a cup of hot water or vegetable stock and add the eggs. Continue to cook gently till the sauce thickens again. Stir in lemon juice before serving with rice.

Goan Egg Curry (*Baida vindālū*)

4 cloves garlic
1 inch (2·5 cm) piece ginger
½ teaspoon paprika or chilli powder
1 teaspoon salt
1 teaspoon cumin seeds
vinegar

4 tablespoons ghee
2 onions, finely chopped
2 inch (5 cm) piece cinnamon, broken
1 tablespoon soft brown sugar
1 teaspoon garam masala
8 hard-boiled eggs, halved

Grind the garlic, ginger, paprika, salt and cumin seeds with a little vinegar to make a paste. Heat ghee and lightly fry the onion. Add cinnamon and the masala paste and fry for two minutes. Stir in sugar, garam masala and a cup of vinegar. Put in the eggs and simmer gently till the sauce is thick. Serve hot with rice or breads.

Spiced Omelette (*Khagina*)

6 eggs
4 tablespoons gram flour
 (besan)
2 tablespoons yogurt
½ teaspoon ground black pepper
1 teaspoon salt

1 teaspoon coriander powder
4 cardamoms, skinned and
 ground
½ cup finely chopped onion
ghee or butter for frying

Beat the eggs and beat in the rest of the ingredients to form a batter. Make into omelettes in the usual way or cook the whole mixture till nearly set. Turn over half and cook for a few seconds. Turn again to a quarter the size and tip out almost immediately. The layered omelette is served cut into thick slices. Garnish with a pinch of garam masala, chilli powder and chopped coriander leaf.

Scrambled Eggs

Many centuries ago, the Parsis fled from their original home of Persia, in the wake of religious persecution. These followers of Zoroaster finally settled in India, especially in the regions of Gujerat and Maharashtra. Parsis have a particular cuisine of their own which includes a number of egg dishes. Here is a Parsi recipe for scrambled eggs which is also cooked in a similar way in Nepal:

2 lbs (1 kilo) potatoes, fried to
 accompany
ghee or oil for frying
8 eggs
1 onion, chopped
1 clove garlic, finely chopped
1 inch 2·5 (cm) piece ginger,
 finely chopped

1 teaspoon turmeric powder
1 teaspoon salt
½ teaspoon paprika or chilli
 powder
2 green chillies, chopped
 (optional)
4 tomatoes, sliced

Cut potatoes in pieces and fry till golden. Meanwhile beat the eggs. Heat 2 tablespoons ghee and fry the onion, stir in the rest of the ingredients and fry for two minutes. Add the beaten eggs and stir till the eggs are set. Serve garnished with a little chopped coriander leaf and surround with the fried potatoes and sliced tomatoes.

Nepali Spiced Eggs

2 tablespoons ghee
1 teaspoon cumin powder
4 cardamoms, skinned and
  ground
½ teaspoon paprika or chilli
  powder

2 cups yogurt
2 tablespoons chopped
  coriander leaves
juice of 1 lemon
8 hard-boiled eggs, halved

Heat ghee and lightly fry the spices for a few minutes. Beat the yogurt till smooth and stir in the coriander leaves, lemon juice and fried spices. Put in the eggs and mix well. Serve cold as a salad, with chopped tomatoes or as a side dish or chutney (achar) for a curry.

Parsi Potato Omelette

4 tablespoons ghee
4 potatoes, diced
1 onion, finely chopped
1 teaspoon salt
½ teaspoon paprika or chilli
  powder

½ teaspoon turmeric powder
1 tablespoon chopped
  coriander leaves
6 eggs

Heat ghee and fry the potatoes and onion till the onion begins to turn golden. Stir in the salt, paprika, turmeric and coriander leaf. Beat the eggs. In a separate pan put a little ghee or butter and a portion of the potato mixture. Pour on some of the beaten egg and gently fry as an omelette. Serve hot or cold. Cold potato omelettes make a nice summer snack when a full meal is not required. Peas, tomatoes or other finely chopped vegetables may be used in the recipe. Cook with the potato and onion.

Stuffed Eggs

For the sauce:

1 tablespoon ghee
1 onion, finely chopped
½ lb (225 g) tomatoes, chopped
1 tablespoon chopped
 coriander leaves

½ teaspoon garam masala
½ teaspoon paprika or chilli
 powder
½ teaspoon salt

For the eggs:

6 hard-boiled eggs
1 tablespoon gram flour
 (besan)
1 tablespoon ghee

1 green chilli, finely chopped
 (optional)
½ teaspoon salt

Prepare the sauce by heating ghee and frying the onion (keep a tablespoonful back for the egg stuffing). Add the tomatoes and the rest of the sauce ingredients. Cook till a thick gravy is formed, adding water if necessary. Meanwhile halve the eggs and remove the yolks. Mash the yolks with besan and a little water to form a paste. Heat ghee and fry the onion, chilli and salt. Add the paste and fry for two minutes. Fill the egg whites with this stuffing. Put the eggs in the sauce and heat through. Serve hot with chapatis or other bread.

Curd (Yogurt)

Curd is now internationally recognised as a health food *par excellence* In those areas of the world where longevity and good health are common, curd in its various forms is a vital part of the people's diet. This nutritious milk food also makes two easily digested cheeses and is an ingredient in sweetmeats. It may be taken plain like a chutney with the food or made into one of the interesting side dishes listed below. Raitas are India's gift to lovers of salad and are also a pleasing and complementary accompaniment to a hotter or spicier dish.

Spiced Curd (*Raita*)

1 tablespoon ghee
2 cloves garlic, finely chopped
½ teaspoon turmeric powder
½ teaspoon salt
2 cups yogurt

½ teaspoon paprika or chilli
   powder
1 tablespoon chopped coriander
   leaf

Heat ghee and fry the garlic, turmeric and salt for two minutes. Beat the yogurt till smooth and stir in paprika and coriander leaf. Cook gently for another five minutes. Chill and serve as a chutney with rice and curry. Any finely cut vegetables can be added to this basic recipe. Garam masala may be substituted for the turmeric.

Cucumber and Curd (*Khira raita*)

2 cups yogurt
pinch of salt
½ teaspoon paprika or chilli
   powder

pinch of cumin powder
1 teaspoon chopped coriander
   leaves
½ lb (225 g) cucumber, grated

Beat curd till smooth. Beat in the seasonings, adding grated cucumber last. Serve chilled.

The Persians have invented many cooling dishes. This cucumber raita can be traced back to Persia where it is also made like this:

2 cups yogurt
½ lb (225 g) cucumber, finely
   chopped
1 spring onion, finely chopped
1 teaspoon chopped fresh mint

1 teaspoon chopped fresh basil
2 tablespoons sultanas
2 tablespoons chopped
   walnuts or pistachio nuts
½ teaspoon salt

Beat the yogurt till smooth and beat in the rest of the ingredients. Serve chilled.

Banana and Curd (*Kela raita*)

2 cups yogurt
¼ teaspoon salt
pinch black pepper
3 bananas, sliced

1 green chilli, finely chopped
   (optional)
chopped coriander leaves

Beat the yogurt with salt and pepper till smooth. Add the bananas and chilli. Garnish with coriander leaf and serve chilled.

Onion and Curd *(Dahi kachūmbar)*

2 cups yogurt
2 onions, finely chopped
1 tomato, chopped
2 green chillies, finely chopped
  (optional)

½ inch (15 mm) piece ginger,
  finely chopped
1 teaspoon salt
1 dessertspoon chopped
  coriander leaf

Beat the yogurt till smooth and beat in the rest of the ingredients.
Serve chilled.

Spiced Potato Salad *(Ālū raita)*

1 lb (450 g) potatoes
½ lb (225 g) tomatoes, sliced
2 cups yogurt
½ teaspoon cumin seeds or
  powder

½ teaspoon salt
pinch black pepper
pinch of chilli powder
chopped coriander leaves

Boil the potatoes, cool, peel and slice. Mix with the tomatoes in a
bowl. Beat the yogurt till smooth, add cumin, salt and pepper and
pour over the potatoes and tomatoes. Sprinkle with chilli powder
and coriander leaf. Serve chilled.

Banana and Cottage Cheese Salad
(Kela chenna)

4 bananas
pinch of salt
pinch of paprika

pinch of garam masala
1 cup chenna or cottage cheese
chopped coriander leaves

Peel and slice the bananas. Mix the seasonings with the chenna and
lay over the banana. Sprinkle with the coriander leaf.

Curd Curry (*Dahi kari*)

½ cup grated coconut
1 teaspoon cumin seeds
1 clove garlic
½ teaspoon paprika or chilli
   powder
1 teaspoon turmeric powder
1 tablespoon chopped
   coriander leaf

2 tablespoons ghee
1 onion, finely chopped
4 tablespoons gram flour
   (besan)
2 cups yogurt
1 teaspoon salt
1 teaspoon garam masala

Grind the coconut, cumin, garlic, paprika, turmeric and coriander leaf to a paste. Heat ghee and lightly fry the onion. Add the masala paste and fry for two minutes. Stir in the flour, yogurt, and salt. Cook gently till the curry thickens and stir in the garam masala. Serve hot with pulau rice. The flavour of this curry can be made more tart by adding a tablespoon of lemon juice with the garam masala.

Curd curry is sometimes made with pakoris (fried savoury gram flour drops). The pakoris are first deep-fried and then allowed to cook in the curry before serving. (See recipe for Pakoras)

Curd Cutlets (*Dahi tikki*)

1 cup yogurt
2 tablespoons gram flour
   (besan)
½ teaspoon salt
½ teaspoon paprika or chilli
   powder
½ teaspoon garam masala
ghee for frying

1 onion, finely chopped
1 tablespoon green peas
½ inch (15 mm) piece ginger,
   finely chopped
10 pistachio nuts, chopped
12 almonds or cashew nuts,
   chopped
2 tablespoons sultanas

Drain the yogurt overnight to get rid of the excess water. Mix in the besan, salt, paprika and garam masala. Mix well, adding extra flour if necessary to make a stiff consistency. Divide into eight portions. Now prepare the filling by lightly frying the onion in a tablespoon of ghee. Add peas, ginger and a pinch of salt. Cook for two minutes, add the nuts and sultanas and fry for a further few minutes till golden.

Make a depression in the yogurt portions and put in some filling. Close up and shape into round flat cakes with the help of a little besan flour. Gently fry in ghee till golden. Serve with vegetables and chutney.

Lentil Cakes in Curd (*Dahi bara*)

1 lb (450 g) lentils
1 inch (2·5 cm) piece ginger
ghee for frying
3 cups yogurt
½ teaspoon salt

½ teaspoon paprika or chilli
 powder
½ teaspoon garam masala
1 teaspoon mustard seeds

Soak the dal overnight. Drain and grind with ginger and a little water to make a thick consistency. Shape into small balls, with the help of a little besan flour, flatten and fry in ghee till golden. Remove, drain and place in a dish. Beat the yogurt till smooth. Stir in the salt, paprika and garam masala. Fry the mustard seeds in a tablespoon of ghee till they begin to jump and stir into the yogurt. Pour over the baras and allow to cool. Serve cold.

Curd Cheese Balls (*Panir kofta*)

6 oz (170 g) panir (stiff curd
 cheese)
1 tablespoon gram flour
 (besan)
½ teaspoon salt
½ teaspoon paprika
½ teaspoon garam masala
1 tablespoon ghee
1 onion, finely chopped

10 almonds or cashew nuts,
 chopped
10 pistachio nuts, chopped
½ inch (15 mm) piece ginger,
 finely chopped
1 green chilli, finely chopped
 (optional)
1 tablespoon chopped
 coriander leaves

For the sauce:

1 tablespoon ghee
2 teaspoons coriander powder
1 teaspoon cumin powder
1 teaspoon poppy seeds

1 tablespoon tomato purée
½ teaspoon soft brown sugar
½ teaspoon salt
2 cups hot water

Mash the panir and knead in the flour, salt, paprika and garam masala. Form into 10–15 small balls. Prepare the filling by frying half of the onion in a tablespoon of ghee. Stir in the almonds, pistachios, half of the ginger, chilli and coriander leaf. Fry till the nuts turn golden. Make a depression in each ball and put in some filling. Close up and serve in the tomato sauce. Prepare the sauce by frying the rest of the onion in a tablespoon of ghee with the rest of the ginger. Stir in the coriander, cumin and poppy seeds. Add the rest of the ingredients and simmer for a few minutes. Put in the koftas and continue simmering till they are well warmed through.

Savouries

These dishes may be included in a teatime menu or may be part of a lunch, dinner or even breakfast. They are useful in providing appetising food where a full meal is not required. Some, such as chevda, are ideal accompaniments for drinks. All the savoury recipes here require cooking though many snacks can of course be prepared without. On a hot day, it is a welcome sight in India to see the man who sells melons and cucumbers, some cut open and sprinkled with salt, chilli and other spices or a few drops of lime juice. A few hot samosas, on the other hand, will cheer up a wintry teatime in the West.

Stuffed Pasties (*Samosa*)

$1\frac{1}{2}$ cups plain flour (maida)
ghee for frying
2 potatoes, medium size
1 small onion, finely chopped

$\frac{1}{2}$ inch (15 mm) piece ginger,
  finely chopped
1 cup green peas or finely
  chopped mixed vegetables

1 teaspoon salt	1 tablespoon chopped
1 teaspoon coriander powder	coriander leaves
½ teaspoon paprika or chilli	½ teaspoon garam masala
powder	1 dessertspoon lemon juice

Sieve the flour with a pinch of salt. Rub in 2 tablespoons melted ghee. Add enough water (5 tablespoons) to make a smooth dough. Knead for ten minutes, cover with a damp cloth and allow to stand. Boil the potatoes, cool, peel and dice or mash. Heat 2 tablespoons ghee and fry the onion. Stir in ginger, peas, salt, coriander powder, paprika and fry for two minutes. Add the cooked potatoes, coriander leaf, garam masala and lemon juice. Fry for a few more minutes and allow to cool. Knead the dough again and make into 20–24 balls, rolling out each one quite thin. Cut in half and lay the pieces over each other. Press lightly together, roll as thin as possible to make a semicircle. Put a portion of the filling on one half of the pastry, moisten the edges and fold the other half over. Press the edges well together and deep fry in hot ghee till crisp and lightly golden. Serve with a chutney. The pastry may be made more flaky by rolling out and adding 2 more tablespoons of ghee. Roll up again and knead. Samosas are useful for using up small quantities of vegetables and the stuffing can be varied to suit.

Savoury Fritters (*Pakora*)

When this batter is used plain to make small deep-fried batter drops, they are known as *pakoris* and served in curd (*Raita pakori*). Any chopped vegetables, especially onion, can be used to make small tasty fritters.

4 tablespoons gram flour	¼ teaspoon chilli powder
(besan)	¼ teaspoon garam masala
1 teaspoon salt	ghee for deep-frying
1 teaspoon baking powder	

Sieve the flour and other ingredients into a mixing bowl and gradually stir in water till a creamy batter is made. Prepare the vegetables by washing and chopping into small pieces. Dip in the batter and fry in hot ghee till golden all over, or put the vegetables in the bowl of batter and drop in spoonfuls of this mixture into the hot ghee or oil. Serve hot or warm for tea with some mint chutney.

Savoury Cakes (*Matthi*)

3 cups plain flour (maida)	3 tablespoons ghee
2 teaspoons salt	2 tablespoons yogurt
2 teaspoons cumin seeds	ghee or oil for deep-frying

Sift the flour with the salt and cumin seeds. Rub in the melted ghee. Mix in the yogurt and enough hot water (about 2 tablespoons) to make a stiff pastry dough. Break off balls of dough and shape to make about 25. Roll out like thick biscuits. Heat the oil and fry each matthi slowly on both sides till golden but not dark. Serve cold for teatime. Decorative shapes can be made by rolling the dough out first and cutting out the matthis with pastry shapes. Matthis will keep like a biscuit in an airtight tin.

Semolina Cakes (*Sūji karkaria*)

1 cup semolina (suji)	2 eggs, beaten (optional)
2 cups milk	10 white cardamoms,
1 tablespoon ghee	skinned and ground
5 tablespoons sugar	ghee or oil for deep-frying

Mix the semolina in a saucepan with the milk, adding the milk gradually to make sure that no lumps are formed. Stir in the melted ghee and sugar. Boil till the mixture thickens, stirring constantly to prevent sticking. Allow the thick mixture to cool and mix in the eggs and cardamom. Heat the oil and fry spoonfuls of semolina mixture till golden on both sides. Remove and drain. Serve the karkarias cold for tea.

Semolina Patties (*Sūji tikki*)

ghee for frying	1 teaspoon turmeric powder
1 cup semolina (suji)	gram or plain flour
1 teaspoon salt	
1 tablespoon chopped	
coriander leaves	

Heat 2 tablespoons ghee, add the semolina and lightly fry for three minutes. Add 2 cups water and salt and continue cooking till the mixture thickens, stirring to prevent sticking. When nearly cooked, mix in the coriander and turmeric. Turn the mixture onto a greased plate and allow to cool. Form portions of the mixture into small patties, roll in flour and fry in hot ghee till golden. Drain and serve. Suji tikkis can be made sweet by substituting sugar for the salt, ground cardamom seeds for the turmeric and chopped nuts for the coriander. Roll in plain flour and serve the drained tikkis sprinkled with a little sugar, ground cardamom and nuts.

Pea and Potato Patties (*Matar ālū tikki*)

1 lb (450 g) potatoes
2 tablespoons wholewheat flour (ata)
1 cup green peas
ghee for frying
2 tablespoons grated coconut
2 green chillies, chopped (optional)
2 tablespoons chopped coriander leaves
½ teaspoon turmeric powder
1 teaspoon salt
½ teaspoon paprika or chilli powder
juice of ½ lemon
semolina

Boil the potatoes, peel and mash. Knead in the flour. Boil the peas and mash. Fry them in 2 tablespoons ghee with the coconut, chillies, coriander, turmeric, salt and paprika. Stir for a few minutes and remove from the heat. Sprinkle with lemon juice and mix well. Divide the mashed potato into walnut-sized balls, flatten on a floured board and place a little of the pea mixture on each. Shape up into small balls and roll in semolina. To make patties, flatten the balls before rolling in semolina. Fry in hot ghee till golden. Serve hot or cold.

Stuffed Puris (*Kachori*)

For stuffed puris make the dough in the same way as for puris. *Dāl bhari pūri* is stuffed with a spicy gram mixture:

4 oz (113 g) split green peas (mung dal)
4 oz (113 g) split yellow peas (channa dal)

4 cloves	½ teaspoon cumin seeds
8 peppercorns	ghee
4 green cardamoms, skinned	1 teaspoon salt

Soak the dals overnight. Drain and grind to make a paste. Grind the cloves, peppercorns, cardamoms and cumin seeds. Heat a table-spoon of ghee and fry the dal paste, ground masala and salt. Knead the ata dough and divide into balls. Flatten and put in a portion of dal filling. Close up and roll into a thick puri. Deep fry in ghee till it begins to turn golden.

Stuffed Puri, Sev *(Sev pūri)*

24 flat crispy puris	1 cup sev (see recipe under
4 boiled potatoes, chopped	Chevda)
1 onion, finely chopped	

Arrange the puris on a dish and cover with a layer of potato. Sprinkle with onion and sev. Serve with a hot chutney, sweet chutney (see under Bhel puri for recipes) and chopped coriander leaves.

This recipe is from Maharashtra.

Stuffed Puri, Potato *(Batāta pūri)*

1 cup yogurt	sweet chutney (as under
24 crispy puris	Bhel puri)
6 boiled potatoes, chopped	cumin powder
salt	coriander leaves, chopped
paprika or chilli powder	
hot chutney (as under	
Bhel puri)	

Beat the yogurt. Arrange the puris on a dish. Make a hole in each and stuff with potatoes. Sprinkle with salt and paprika or chilli powder and hot chutney. Pour curd on each puri and some sweet chutney. Sprinkle with a little cumin powder and coriander leaf. Serve while the puris are still crisp.

Stuffed Puri, Puffed Rice *(Bhel pūri)*

A favourite Maharashtra savoury. Some Bombay restaurants make it a speciality.

For the hot chutney:

½ cup fresh coriander leaves
2 green chillies
1 teaspoon chopped ginger

1 clove garlic
salt to taste

Grind together to make a paste, adding a little water if necessary.

For the sweet chutney:

⅓ cup stoned dates
juice and pulp of 1 lemon
　(or equivalent in tamarind)

salt to taste

Grind together to form a paste.

For the puri:

2 cups puffed rice or Rice
　Krispies
1½ cups sev (see under recipe
　for Chevda)
12 crushed crisp puris

3 boiled potatoes, chopped
1 onion, finely chopped
juice of 1 lemon
1 tomato, chopped
coriander leaves, chopped

Combine the puffed rice, sev, puris, potatoes and onion, mix well with the two chutneys. Sprinkle with lemon juice. Garnish each serving with tomato and coriander leaf and chilli powder to taste. Serve before the puris lose their crispness.

Potato Cutlets *(Ālū tikki)*

1 lb (450 g) potatoes
2 onions, chopped
2 green chillies (optional)
2 cloves garlic
1 dessertspoon gram flour
　(besan)

½ teaspoon cumin seeds
juice of ½ lemon
2 eggs, for binding
ghee for frying

Wash the potatoes and boil with $\frac{1}{2}$ teaspoon salt till tender. Peel and mash. Grind all the ingredients to a paste. Add the potato, mix well and stir in the beaten eggs. Shape into cutlets or balls, roll in flour or bread crumbs and fry on both sides till golden. The eggs may be eliminated as a binder and flour substituted.

Potato Rounds (*Ālū chāt*)

2 lbs (900 g) small potatoes or
  sweet potatoes
4 green chillies, chopped
  (optional)
1 teaspoon garam masala

1 teaspoon cumin powder
juice of 1 lemon (or tamarind
  juice
$1\frac{1}{2}$ teaspoons salt
coriander leaves, chopped

Wash potatoes and boil till tender. Peel and slice into rounds. Put in a bowl and mix with the other ingredients. Serve with a salad.

Mixed fruit chat can be prepared in the same way. Cut up some fresh fruits, mix and add garam masala, cumin powder, chopped green chillies or chilli powder and salt.

Potato Balls in Batter (*Ālū bonda*)

1 lb (450 g) potatoes
ghee
2 onions, finely chopped
2 green chillies, finely chopped
  (optional)
1 inch (2·5 cm) piece ginger,
  finely chopped
a few curry leaves
1 teaspoon mustard seeds

1 tablespoon split black peas
  (urhad dal)
2 tablespoons cashew nuts
1 teaspoon turmeric powder
1 teaspoon salt
juice of $\frac{1}{2}$ lemon
8 oz (225 g) gram flour
  (besan)

Boil potatoes and mash. Heat 3 tablespoons ghee and fry the onions, green chillies, ginger and curry leaves for a few minutes. Add the mustard seeds, urhad dal and cashew nuts and continue frying till the nuts begin to turn golden. Stir in turmeric and salt. Add the potatoes and mix well. Remove from heat, sprinkle with lemon juice and make the mixture into small balls. Make a thick batter from gram flour and water, adding a pinch of chilli powder and salt. Dip the potato balls in batter and deep-fry in ghee or oil till golden.

Masala Upuma

For the masala:
small piece of cinnamon
1 teaspoon coriander seeds
½ teaspoon cumin seeds
1 teaspoon paprika or chilli
  powder
1 teaspoon turmeric powder
ghee
juice of 4 lemons
8 oz (225 g) semolina
2 teaspoons mustard seeds

2 teaspoons split black peas
  (urhad dal)
2 teaspoons split yellow peas
  (channa dal)
2 tablespoons cashew nuts
2 onions, finely chopped
1 tablespoon chopped
  coriander leaves
1 teaspoon salt
4 oz (113 g) grated coconut

Grind the masala ingredients and fry in a tablespoon of ghee. Remove from heat and add the lemon juice. Roast the semolina on a low heat for about five minutes. Heat 4 tablespoons ghee in a pan and fry the mustard seeds, urhad dal, channa dal and cashew nuts. Stir in the onion and fry till golden. Add coriander leaves. Fry for a few minutes and add 2 cups hot water. Stir in salt, coconut and masala mixture. Add the semolina and cook gently till a thick paste is formed, stirring constantly. Serve hot. Upumas come from South India.

Peanut Upuma

12 oz (340 g) peanuts
2 tablespoons ghee
½ teaspoon mustard seeds
4 green chillies, chopped
  (optional)

1 onion, sliced
1 teaspoon turmeric powder
2 tablespoons grated coconut

Boil peanuts till tender and chop. Heat ghee and fry mustard seeds. Add the chillies, onion and turmeric and fry till the onion is golden. Stir in the nuts and coconut and mix well. Serve hot garnished with chopped coriander leaf.

Savoury Puffs *(Gol gappa)*

3 tablespoons plain flour
  (maida)
1 teaspoon split black pea
  flour (urhad dal)
3 tablespoons semolina (suji)
½ teaspoon salt

ghee for deep-frying
cooked Bengal peas
boiled potato, chopped
sonth (see recipe)
jira pāni (see recipe)

Sift together the flours, semolina and salt. Add enough warm water to make a soft dough. Knead for 15 minutes. Cover with a damp cloth and leave to stand for half an hour. Knead again for a few minutes and make up into small walnut-sized balls. Grease the board and roller with ghee and roll out the balls as thin as possible. Keep ready in the damp cloth and deep-fry 3 or 4 at a time in hot ghee. The gappas should puff up and become translucent and golden. Drain. Serve by pressing in a hole and filling each with Bengal peas, cooked potato, ½ teaspoon sonth and 1 teaspoon jira pani (see under Drinks and Soups). Eat before they become soggy. Gol gappas can also be made from plain flour only.

Crispy Flour Discs *(Papri)*

4 oz (113 g) plain flour
3 tablespoons water

ghee

Make a dough of flour and water. Grease the knuckles with ghee and knead for ten minutes. Roll out thin and cut into rounds of about an inch (3 cm) in diameter. Prick with a fork and fry in hot ghee till golden. Serve the papris dipped in sonth (see recipe) and beaten yogurt with Bengal peas and cooked potato. Sprinkle with salt, paprika or chilli powder, garam masala and cumin powder.

Sweet and Sour Sauce *(Sonth)*

10 oz (280 ml) treacle or syrup
4 tablespoons lemon juice or
  tamarind juice

1 teaspoon paprika or chilli
  powder
3 teaspoons salt

1 teaspoon finely chopped
  ginger, crushed
½ teaspoon garam masala

½ teaspoon cumin powder
red colouring

Heat the treacle with lemon juice and paprika. Add the rest of the ingredients and mix thoroughly. Stir in a few drops of colouring to make a brick-red colour. Add a little water if the sauce is too thick. Serve with papris.

Fried Channa Dal Savoury

Like *chevda* and *sev*, this savoury 'nibble' can be served as an appetiser with drinks or as a light snack.

1 cup split yellow peas (channa
  dal)
1 tablespoon sodium
  bicarbonate

ghee
1 teaspoon salt
½ teaspoon garam masala
pinch of chilli powder

Soak the dal all day in water with the soda. Next day drain and allow to dry. Heat ghee or cooking oil in a pan and fry a handful of dal at a time on medium heat. Drain well. Roll all the fried channa in salt, garam masala and chilli powder. Other dals can be prepared in the same way.

Puffed Rice and Nuts Savoury (*Chevda, chūra*)

2 tablespoons ghee
¼ teaspoon turmeric powder
½ teaspoon cumin powder
⅓ cup peanuts
⅓ cup cashew nuts
2 tablespoons raisins
⅓ cup grated coconut

1 teaspoon sesame seeds
1½ cups puffed rice or
  Rice Krispies
1½ teaspoons salt
½ teaspoon paprika or chilli
  powder

Heat ghee and fry the turmeric and cumin for two minutes. Add peanuts, cashew nuts and raisins. Fry for two minutes then stir in the coconut and sesame seeds. Add the rice cereal, salt and paprika or chilli powder. Serve hot or cold.

Chevda and fried channa dal are sometimes mixed with sev. Sev has to be made like vermicelli using a fine-guage Mouli shredder or similar gadget:

2 cups gram flour (besan)
2 teaspoons salt
¼ teaspoon turmeric
   powder

½ teaspoon paprika or chilli
   powder
1 teaspoon garam masala
2 tablespoons ghee

Sift the flour and other ingredients together. Rub in the ghee. Add enough warm water to make a stiff dough and knead for five minutes. Heat ghee or cooking oil in a deep pan. Over the pan, pass the dough through the shredder to form thin strips like vermicelli. Allow to drop in the hot ghee and fry till nearly golden. Remove the sev quickly and drain, adding more strips till the dough is used up.

The Tale of the Sadhu

'The guard was still chuckling when they reached the turning where the merchant had to leave him. "I suppose you supplied some of the ingredients. Well at least you weren't as unlucky as the sadhu." "Sadhu, what sadhu?" questioned the merchant. "I thought everyone knew the story. I heard it as a boy. Well, you see there was a certain holy man who used to sit by the roadside day after day, month after month. The intensity and length of his meditation being the admiration of all. Devout women from the nearby village would come and feed him regularly with rice and a few choicely-cooked vegetables. The sadhu was serenely contented and felt that by all his austerities he now merited asking a boon. "O Lord," he prayed, "I am well fed and happy, yet I long for some sweetmeats—the one thing that the village women never bring me." Feeling sure that his fervent prayer would be answered, the sadhu returned to his meditations. Later, he was aroused by a sharp tug on the shoulder. "Come on, up you get!" shouted a rasping voice. "Just the man we're looking for." The commander was very pleased. His army had been unable to procure a second cook in the village and now his luck had changed. He would be able to provide the promised feast for his valiant soldiers after all. The sadhu was soon put to work preparing sweets and he spent many blistering hours endlessly stirring the great pots of milk and syrup, chopping and pounding hundreds of nuts and grinding various spices. "O Lord," he thought, "how did I know that my prayer would be answered in such a manner!" . . .'

Sweetmeats and Sweet Dishes

Sweetmeats

The Portuguese traveller, Sebastian Manrique, who visited India during the reign of Shahjahan, noted that in Bengal 'Entire streets could be seen wholly occupied by skilled sweet-meat-makers who proved their skill by offering wonderful sweets, scented dainties of all kinds which would stimulate the most jaded appetite to gluttony.' (*Travels of Sebastian Manrique*, Volume II, page 156).

Festival time in India, as in the West, is always sweet time. The prettiest of Indian festivals is probably Dīpāvali or Divāli, the four-day festival of lights. A *dipa* is a lamp and *avali* means a row. Houses are lit up all over with rows of lamps, giving a magical air to any village. Dīpāvali is New Year's Day in the Hindu calendar, the first day of the month of Kartik, which falls in October or November. Divāli is considered an auspicious day and people like to spend the day in a festive mood giving parties and presents. Sweets are some of the favourite presents and families bring out their own special recipes at this time.

Milk Sweet (*Barfi*)

Many varieties of barfi are prepared with *khoya* (dried fresh whole milk) as the basis. Khoya can be made by mixing dried full-cream milk with water. When barfi is formed into balls they are called *dudh pera*.

8 oz (225 g) sugar	8 crushed white cardamoms,
1 cup water	skinned
10 oz (280 g) dried milk	1 tablespoon nuts, chopped

Make a syrup by boiling sugar and water briskly. The syrup is ready when a tiny drop forms a ball when put on the edge of a cold dish. Add the milk powder and crushed cardamom seeds. Mix well and turn out on to a greased dish. Leave to cool. Fashion into individual balls or cut in cubes or diamonds. Top with crushed cardamom seeds, chopped nuts and silver balls. Plain barfi may be enriched by substituting ground nuts for some of the milk and by adding rosewater to the syrup.

Coconut Barfi (*Barfi narial*)

8 oz (225 g) sugar	1 teaspoon rosewater
1 cup water	8 white cardamoms, crushed
6 oz (170 g) dried milk	seeds
3 tablespoons grated coconut	cochineal or yellow colouring

Make a syrup as for plain barfi and mix in the dried milk and coconut. Remove from heat and add rosewater, cardamom and a few drops of colouring. Turn out on to a greased dish.

Pistachio Barfi (*Barfi pistā*)

8 oz (225 g) sugar	12 oz (340 g) pistachio nuts
1 cup water	

Make a syrup as for barfi. Meanwhile pound the nuts and stir into the syrup. Stir till a dry mixture is obtained. Turn on to a greased dish. Decorate with silver balls and cut when cool.

Bombay Halva *(Bambai halva)*

1 cup sugar
pinch of saffron or yellow
  colouring
2 tablespoons milk

2 cups water
3 tablespoons ghee
4 oz (113 g) semolina
2 tablespoons sultanas

Mix the sugar, saffron, milk and water and boil gently for five minutes. Melt ghee in a separate pan and fry the semolina gently for about ten minutes till golden. When the ghee begins to separate from the semolina pour in the syrup. Add the washed sultanas and heat till all the superfluous liquid has been driven off, stirring constantly with a wooden spoon. Turn out on to a greased dish and decorate with crushed cardamom seeds and sliced nuts.

This halva can also be prepared with wholewheat flour (ata) or gram flour (besan). It is often served hot with puris and is a traditional favourite.

Carrot Halva *(Gājar halva)*

1 pint (570 ml) milk
2 lbs (900 g) carrots, grated
5 oz (140 g) soft brown sugar
2 oz (60 g) creamed coconut
  or ghee
2 oz (60 g) ghee

15 white cardamoms, skinned
  and crushed
18 almonds, blanched and
  sliced
red colouring

Boil the milk and carrots on medium heat till the mixture thickens, stirring all the time. Add the sugar and cook for a further fifteen minutes. Now add the creamed coconut and ghee and cook till all has been absorbed and the mixture is thick. Add a few drops of colouring to make the halva a glowing red colour. At this point, 2 tablespoons of sultanas could be added. Turn out on to a greased dish, spread out and decorate with crushed cardamom and nuts. Cut when cool.

Banana Halva (*Kela halva*)

2 tablespoons ghee
5 ripe bananas
5 oz (140 g) soft brown sugar

pinch of saffron or yellow
colouring

Heat the ghee. Peel the bananas and cut in small pieces. Gently fry for five minutes. Mash. Add sugar and ¼ cup of water. Cook gently till the water has been absorbed. Add the saffron or yellow colouring, mix well and turn on to a greased dish. Decorate with crushed cardamom seeds and sliced nuts.

Karachi Halva

This sweet from Sind is the Indian version of Turkish Delight.

20 oz (570 g) sugar
20 oz (570 ml) water
4 oz (113 g) cornflour
yellow colouring
2 teaspoons lemon juice
ghee

10 almonds, blanched and
finely chopped
10 pistachio nuts, finely
chopped
12 white cardamoms, skinned
and crushed

Boil the sugar and water for five minutes. Mix cornflour with a cup of water and stir into the syrup. Add colouring and cook over a medium heat, stirring continuously to prevent catching, till the mixture becomes a jelly-like lump. Add lemon juice and continue stirring till the mixture sticks to the bottom of the pan. Add teaspoonfuls of ghee and continue cooking till the mixture stops sticking to the pan and becomes a lump (about half an hour). Add nuts and cardamom. Turn out on to a greased dish and smooth flat. Cut when set.

Marrow Halva (*Gūda halva*)

1 lb (450 g) peeled and seeded
marrow or pumpkin
½ cup milk
6 oz (170 g) soft brown sugar

1 tablespoon sultanas
1 tablespoon sliced almonds
2 tablespoons ghee

Cut the marrow into small pieces and boil in a pan with the milk for ten minutes, stirring and mashing continuously. Add sugar and continue heating for another eight minutes. Add the sultanas, almonds and ghee and cook for a further five minutes or till the halva is dry. Turn out on to a greased dish and decorate with crushed cardamom seeds.

Rice Halva *(Chāval halva)*

1 lb (450 g) sugar	1 tablespoon rosewater
20 oz (570 ml) water	12 white cardamoms, skinned
3 tablespoons milk	and crushed
4 oz (113 g) rice flour	20 almonds, blanched and
red or yellow colouring	chopped
ghee	10 pistachio nuts, chopped

Boil the sugar in half the water for five minutes. Add milk and boil for another five minutes. Remove from heat. Dissolve rice flour in the rest of the water and stir into the syrup. Cook on a medium heat, adding a few drops of colouring, stirring continuously. Add teaspoons of ghee to prevent the mixture sticking to the pan. Add rosewater and half of the cardamom and nuts. When the mixture forms a lump turn out on to a greased dish, flatten and decorate with the rest of the cardamom and nuts. Cut when cool.

Sultana Halva *(Kishmish halva)*

1 cup melted ghee	½ cup water
2 cups sultanas	1 tablespoon rosewater
2 cups sugar	

Heat ghee and fry the sultanas. Remove from heat and mash. Boil sugar and water for five minutes. Add the sultana paste and rosewater and cook till the syrup is absorbed. Turn on to a greased dish and allow to cool.

Green Lentil Halva (*Mūng dāl halva*)

8 oz (225 g) split green peas
  (mung dal)
4 tablespoons ghee
1 tablespoon raisins or sultanas
1 pint (570 ml) milk
8 oz (225 g) sugar

pinch of saffron
6 white cardamoms, skinned
  and crushed
10 almonds, blanched and
  sliced

Soak dal overnight. Drain and grind. Fry in ghee till golden. Add raisins, milk, sugar and saffron. Cook on a low heat, stirring till the liquid is absorbed and the ghee separates out. Turn on to a greased dish. Decorate with cardamom and nuts. Serve hot.

Peanut Halva (*Phali halva*)

1 lb (450 g) peanuts
1 cup ghee
5 oz (140 g) sugar
6 white cardamoms, skinned
  and crushed

pinch of saffron or yellow
  colouring
2 tablespoons raisins

Soak the peanuts in water for an hour. Drain and grind to a paste. Add to the rest of the ingredients and cook gently, stirring to prevent sticking, till the mixture thickens. Turn on to a greased dish and decorate with sliced almonds. Cut when cool.

Beetroot Halva (*Chukunda halva*)

4 beetroots, cooked
1 cup sugar
4 tablespoons ghee
2 tablespoons cashew nuts,
  chopped

2 tablespoons raisins
10 white cardamoms, skinned
  and crushed

Mash the cooked beetroots and gently cook with the sugar till the mixture thickens. Add teaspoons of ghee and keep stirring till a lump is formed. Add the nuts, raisins and cardamoms. Turn on to a greased dish. Colouring can be added along with the ghee.

Gram Flour Balls (*Laddū besan*)

In August or September, Ganesh Chaturthi, the festival of Ganesh or Ganapati, the elephant-headed god, is celebrated. This has become the most spectacular event in the Bombay area. Laddus, sweets made from gram flour, are offered to the image of the god of plenty in memory of the story of his creation. Lord Shiva's wife, Parvati, took an oil bath and rubbed the oil from her body with the aid of gram flour. She then modelled the figure of a child from the lumps of oil-saturated flour. She placed the child outside the bathroom where he was later encountered by Shiva. The child, Ganesh, would not allow Shiva to enter the bathroom who thereupon angrily slashed off the child's head. Shiva searched in vain for the head to console his weeping wife and he eventually substituted the head of an elephant. Ganesh later performed many good deeds and is now worshipped as the god of success, particularly by business men.

4 tablespoons ghee
8 oz (225 g) gram flour (besan)
6 white cardamoms, skinned and crushed
8 oz (225 g) soft brown sugar
2 tablespoons pistachio nuts, chopped

Heat ghee and gradually add the flour. Fry till brown. Remove from heat and add the cardamom, sugar and nuts. Mix well, allow to cool and form into balls, with the help of a little ghee if necessary.

Semolina Balls (*Laddū sūji*)

4 tablespoons ghee
8 oz (225 g) semolina
8 oz (225 g) soft brown sugar
½ pint (280 ml) milk
1 tablespoon cashew nuts, chopped
1 tablespoon raisins or sultanas

Heat ghee and gently fry the semolina till it begins to turn golden. When the ghee begins to separate out, add sugar and milk and continue cooking till the mixture thickens. Add the nuts and raisins. Remove from the heat, allow to cool and form into small balls. Sprinkle with powdered cardamom.

Cheese Fudge (Sandesh)

3 pints (1700 ml) fresh milk
1½ cups yogurt
1 cup sugar

cardamoms and nuts for
decoration

Heat the milk till it boils. Turn down the heat and add the yogurt, cooking gently till lumps are formed. Strain the panir into a muslin bag and press with a weight for half an hour. Chop the panir and cook gently in a separate pan with the sugar, stirring well. When fairly thick remove from heat and turn on to a dish. Decorate with crushed cardamom seeds and chopped nuts. Cut when cold.

Flour and Milk Cakes (Pinni)

4 tablespoons ghee
4 oz (113 g) wholewheat flour (ata)
6 oz (170 g) soft brown sugar

2 oz (60 g) full-cream powdered milk
1 tablespoon sultanas
1 tablespoon chopped nuts

Heat ghee and gently fry the flour for about fifteen minutes. Add the sugar. Make the powdered milk into a thick paste with a little hot water and stir into the flour and sugar. Add the sultanas and nuts and mix well. Form into flattened balls and sprinkle with powdered cardamom seed.

Milk Balls in Rosewater Syrup (Gulāb jāman)

8 oz (225 g) full-cream powdered milk
1 tablespoon plain flour
1 tablespoon baking powder
milk

ghee for deep-frying
1 cup sugar
2 cups water
2 tablespoons rosewater

Sift together the milk powder, flour and baking powder. Add enough milk (10–12 tablespoons) to make a soft, stiff dough. Leave to stand for an hour. Form the dough into walnut-sized balls. Heat ghee and slowly deep-fry the balls till golden all over. The ghee should not be too hot or the balls will only cook on the outside. Meanwhile make a syrup by boiling the sugar and water for a few minutes. Add rosewater. Put the drained jamans in the hot syrup and allow to soak for a few hours before serving. This is a favourite after-dinner or teatime sweet.

Nuts, cardamom seeds or small pieces of sugar candy can be inserted in the balls before cooking. Yogurt can be used to make the dough instead of milk, giving a tarter flavour. A nuttier consistency can be obtained by using 4 oz (113 g) ground almonds and 4 oz (113 g) plain flour instead of milk powder. Combine with the baking powder and rub in 2 tablespoons of ghee. Make up the dough with yogurt and cook as above.

Sugar-Coated Cubes (*Shakar pāre*)

1 cup sugar
1 cup water
1 cup plain flour
1 tablespoon ghee

2 teaspoons ground almonds
1 tablespoon yogurt
ghee or cooking oil for frying

Make a syrup by boiling the sugar and water for about eight minutes, keep on one side. Sift the flour and rub in a tablespoon of heated ghee. Add the ground almonds, mix well and gradually add yogurt to make a smooth ball. Knead well and roll out. Cut up to make cubes the size of sugar lumps. Deep-fry handfuls of cubes till golden. Drain and drop into the syrup. Take each batch out and keep in a shallow dish. Finally pour any remaining syrup over the cubes and allow to cool.

Sugar-Coated Doughnuts (*Bālu shāhi*)

8 oz (225 g) plain flour
1 teaspoon baking powder
ghee
yogurt
1 cup sugar
1 cup water

1 tablespoon rosewater
1 tablespoon blanched almonds
    chopped
1 tablespoon pistachio nuts,
    chopped

Sift the flour and baking powder together and rub in 3 tablespoons melted ghee. Add enough warm yogurt to form a soft dough. Knead

136

well and make into 12–16 balls. Gently flatten each ball and make a depression in the centre. Heat ghee and gently deep-fry the dough-nuts till they turn golden and swell up. Remove and drain. Mean-while make up a thick syrup by boiling sugar and water as for shakar pare and stir in the rosewater. Arrange the doughnuts on a dish and pour the syrup over them. Decorate with nuts and silver balls. Balu shahi, like shakar pare, are made in the Punjab.

Semolina and Coconut-Milk Cakes (*Kalkals*)

Milk of 1 coconut
2 cups semolina
1 teaspoon salt
2–3 eggs

ghee for deep frying
1 cup sugar
1 cup water

Extract the milk from the flesh of the coconut. Sift the semolina and salt together and add the coconut milk. Beat the eggs and grad-ually add to form a soft dough. Form into small cakes with the help of a little ghee on the hands. Deep-fry in ghee till golden. Next day make up a thick syrup as for shakar pare. Put in the kalkals and continue heating gently till the syrup dries and they are well frosted with sugar. This recipe is from Maharashtra.

Thick Milk (*Khoya*) Cake

1 cup sugar
1 cup water
12 oz (340 g) full-cream milk
 powder
½ teaspoon tartaric acid powder

1 tablespoon blanched
 almonds, chopped
1 tablespoon pistachio nuts,
 chopped

Boil the sugar and water for five minutes. Mix in the milk powder, tartaric acid and nuts and heat gently till all the liquid is absorbed. Turn out into a greased tin and allow to set. Decorate with silver balls or other cake decorations.

Curd Balls in Syrup (*Rasgullas*)

4 cups full-cream milk
juice of 2 lemons
1 tablespoon plain flour

1 cup sugar
2 cups water
1 tablespoon rosewater

Heat the milk to boiling and add the lemon juice to curdle. When completely curdled pour into a muslin bag and allow to drain. When almost dry press the bag with a weight and leave to drain further. Once the solid chenna has been formed, add flour and knead to a soft dough. Form into small balls. Boil sugar and water for five minutes to make a syrup and carefully drop in the balls. Cook the balls gently in the syrup for fifteen minutes. Cool and add rosewater. Serve chilled in the syrup.

Cheese Balls in Cream (*Ras malai*)

Ras malai are flattened balls of chenna soaked in a mixture of thickened fresh milk and double cream (malai). This is served as a dessert or on its own in the Punjab.

4 cups full-cream milk and
    enough for soaking the
    rasgullas
juice of 2 lemons
1 tablespoon plain flour
1 cup double cream
2 teaspoons pistachio nuts,
    finely chopped

3 teaspoons blanched almonds,
    finely chopped
sugar
2 cups water
1 tablespoon rosewater

Make rasgullas as in the previous recipe. Prepare a filling of 1 tablespoon double cream, 1 teaspoon of pounded pistachios, 1 teaspoon of pounded almonds and 2 teaspoons sugar. Flatten the balls, make a depression in each and fill with the mixture. Roll up again. Make a syrup as above and gently cook the balls in it for ten minutes. Remove and leave to soak in milk for 3–4 hours. Remove and drain, keeping the milk to make rabri. Heat the milk till it is reduced to half the quantity. Add the rest of the double cream and bring to the boil. Pour over the rasgullas. Sprinkle with rosewater and the rest of the nuts. Serve chilled.

Flour Spirals in Syrup (*Jalebi*)

1½ cups plain flour
2 tablespoons yogurt
1 teaspoon saffron or yellow or
   orange colouring (optional)

2 cups sugar
2 cups water
ghee or oil for deep-frying

Sieve the flour into a basin and add the curd and enough water (about a cup) to make a thick batter. Beat in the saffron or colouring and allow to stand in a warm place overnight. Boil sugar and water for ten minutes to make a thick syrup. Keep warm. Beat the batter again. Heat ghee in a deep frying pan and fill a small funnel, or coconut shell with a hole in, with batter. Keep a finger over the hole and hold over the hot ghee. Remove the finger and move the stream of batter so that a spiral a little bigger than a cup in diameter is formed. Fry till golden on both sides, remove and drain and allow to soak in the syrup. Remove the jalebis and pile them in a dish. Serve hot or cold.

Jalebis are a favourite with children and can be served soaked in milk. Sometimes they are cooked in a custard or in a milk pudding like semolina.

Mysore Sweetmeat (*Masūr ki pak*)

6 tablespoons ghee
2 tablespoons gram flour
   (besan) or plain flour
   (maida)
10 almonds, blanched and
   ground

20 almonds, blanched and
   chopped
6 cardamoms, skinned and
   ground
1 cup sugar
½ cup water

Melt 4 tablespoons ghee in a pan. Sieve the flour into the ghee and fry gently for five minutes, stirring in the ground almonds and cardamom. Meanwhile, mix the sugar and water and boil till a thick syrup is formed. Pour over the flour and mix. Gradually add the rest of the ghee, stirring continuously. The sweet is ready when it becomes thick and spongy. Spread on a dish and decorate with the chopped almonds. When nearly cold cut in squares or diamonds.

Semolina Cookies (*Nān khatai*)

4 tablespoons ghee or butter
4 tablespoons sugar
1 cup semolina

6 cardamoms, skinned and
 ground
chopped nuts for decoration

Beat the ghee and sugar together till creamy. Sieve in the semolina
and cardamom and beat well. Leave the mixture for half an hour.
Knead well and shape into small flat cakes. Decorate with chopped
or grated nuts and place on a greased tin in an oven at Regulo 5 or
6 (325°F/163°C) for about half an hour till golden. They can be stored
in a tin like biscuits.

Sweet-Potato Balls (*Susiam*)

½ lb (225 g) sweet potatoes
2 cardamoms, skinned and
 ground
4 oz (113 g) soft brown sugar
 or jaggery

1 tablespoon grated coconut
½ teaspoon salt
2 tablespoons rice flour
¼ teaspoon turmeric powder
ghee or oil for deep-frying

Boil the potatoes till tender. Peel and mash. Mix in the cardamom,
sugar, coconut and salt. Mix well and shape into small balls. Mix
flour, turmeric and a pinch of salt with enough water to make a
thick batter (about 3 tablespoons). Dip the balls in the batter and fry
in hot ghee or oil. Serve hot. These sweet and savoury balls come from
South India.

Flour Rolls in Syrup (*Kalkas*)

1 coconut (or equivalent
 creamed coconut)
1 cup plain flour (maida)
ghee for deep-frying

1 teaspoon powdered
 cardamom seeds
2 cups sugar
1 cup water

Grate the coconut and extract the milk. Mix flour with the milk and
knead to form a soft dough. Make small balls of dough, flatten with
a fork and roll off to form little rolls. Heat ghee and fry the rolls till

golden. Drain and put in a bowl. Sprinkle with cardamom. Make a thick syrup by boiling the sugar and water for ten minutes. Pour over the fried rolls. Serve hot or cold.

Black-Eye Beans and Coconut

2 cups black-eye beans
½ teaspoon salt
1 coconut

soft brown sugar
lemon juice

Pour boiling water over the beans to cover and leave to soak overnight. Boil the beans with salt till soft. Drain and allow to cool. Meanwhile, grate the coconut and stir into the beans. Sprinkle with sugar to taste and mix well. Serve cold with a sprinkling of lemon juice.

Coconut and Raisin Sweet (*Lethri*)

4 tablespoons sugar
2 tablespoons water
yolk of an egg (for decoration
   —optional)
1 coconut, grated
2 slices bread, crusts removed
   and crumbled

2 tablespoons almonds or
   cashew nuts, finely chopped
2 tablespoons sultanas
1 tablespoon rosewater

Melt the sugar in the water on a low heat. Beat the egg-yolk. Pour the beaten yolk onto the melted sugar to form a floral pattern. Lift the yolk out of the pan and place on a plate. Add the coconut, bread, nuts and sultanas to the sugar. Mix thoroughly and cook gently till the ingredients are well mixed, stirring to prevent sticking. Add a tablespoon of rosewater. When the mixture has reached a sticky toffee consistency, pour onto the plate on top of the egg-yolk. Press to breadslice thickness with a buttered rolling pin. When set, turn the plate over to serve and cut in squares. The yellow egg yolk will form a decoration on top of the lethri.

This recipe is from Goa.

Date and Nut Sweet

1 lb (450 g) dried stoned dates
2 tablespoons almonds or other
  nuts, blanched and sliced
1 teaspoon fennel seeds or
  aniseed

1 teaspoon crushed cardamom
  seeds

Flatten the dates with the fingers and roll out to make a thin sheet. Press in the almonds and fennel seeds, sprinkle with cardamom powder. Cut in squares to serve.

Dried apricots can be treated in a similar way. A variant of this date and nut sweet is to cut open whole dates, remove the stone and substitute a nut and a sprinkling of cardamom powder. Close up and cover with a thin envelope of marzipan.

Sweet Dishes

Sweet Rice (*Mīthe chāval*)

Indian 'rice pudding' is served on festive occasions in Kashmir and served in small shallow earthenware pots. Children often find the best part of the pudding is the skin on the top and the caught layer on the bottom which has to be scraped off to be eaten. In Kashmir the pudding is deliberately treated to produce these effects by setting the pot on hot coals and piling them on the lid. English housewives may already be familiar with the technique which may occur quite accidentally!

1 cup rice	24 almonds, blanched and
1 cup sugar	chopped
1 cup water	2 tablespoons sultanas
6 cups milk	pinch of saffron, pounded in
2 tablespoons ghee or butter	in warm milk
12 white cardamoms	3 tablespoons chopped nuts

Soak the rice. Boil the sugar and water together for five minutes and add milk. Fry the washed and drained rice in ghee for a few minutes till the grains become opaque. Cook in the milk syrup till the rice is tender, adding the cardamoms, almonds, sultanas and saffron. When all the liquid is absorbed, transfer to a medium oven (Regulo 4) for half an hour. Serve sprinkled with the chopped nuts.

Creamed Rice *(Khīr)*

Khir is often given by Hindus to the priests on religious occasions.

1 cup rice
1 tablespoon ghee or butter
2 pints (1135 ml) milk
4 tablespoons sugar
pinch of saffron, pounded in
  a tablespoon of hot milk
1 tablespoon rosewater
1 tablespoon almonds,
  blanched and chopped
1 tablespoon sultanas

Soak the rice in water, wash and drain. Heat ghee and fry the drained rice for a few minutes till the grains become opaque. Add milk and bring to the boil, stirring continuously. Lower the heat and simmer till the rice is tender. Add sugar and saffron. Continue simmering till the rice becomes creamy, stirring all the time. Stir in the rosewater, nuts and sultanas. Serve hot, sprinkled with cardamom powder. Khir may also be served cold.

Creamed Almonds *(Khīr badām)*

4 pints (2270 ml) full-cream
  milk
8 oz (225 g) sugar
12 oz (340 g) almonds, blanched
  and finely chopped
pinch of saffron, pounded in a
  tablespoon hot milk
½ teaspoon powdered
  cardamom seeds

Heat milk in a large pan with sugar and cook till it thickens to form khoya. Stir in almonds, saffron and cardamom powder. Serve hot with fresh hot puris.

This dish is frequently served in South India with sambhar, aviyal and pachadi (see recipes).

Sweet Rice Pulau *(Zarda pulau)*

1½ cups rice
4 tablespoons ghee
6 cloves
6 white cardamoms

small piece cinnamon
8 oz (225 g) sugar
pinch of saffron, pounded in a
  tablespoon hot milk
1 tablespoon sultanas
1 tablespoon rosewater

1 tablespoon almonds,
  blanched and chopped
1 tablespoon pistachio nuts,
  chopped
silver balls or silver leaf

Wash the rice and leave to soak. Drain. Heat ghee and gently fry the cloves, cardamoms and cinnamon for two minutes. Add the rice and continue frying till the grains become opaque. Pour on 3 cups hot water and cook like a pulau till the rice is soft. Add sugar and saffron. Mix well and stir in the sultanas, rosewater and half the nuts. Serve hot or cold.

This recipe was known as Zardbiranj in the seventeenth century. In Nepal it is sometimes served topped with soft brown sugar and cream.

Tamil Sweet Rice (*Phakkarai pongal*)

Pongal means 'boiled rice' in Tamil and the word gives its name to the Pongal festival which lasts for three days. During Pongal, khir is prepared from rice, milk and jaggery to be offered to Indra, who rules over the kingdom of the gods. This is served for breakfast. On the third day of Pongal the sacred cattle are fed with a thick rice gruel made with sugar-cane juice, after having been washed, groomed, painted and garlanded with flowers. People try to marry during the auspicious six months following Pongal and quantities of rice may be included in the bride's dowry.

2 cups rice
1 cup split green peas (mung
  dal)
2 pints (1135 ml) milk
2 cups jaggery, soft brown
  sugar or treacle

1 tablespoon raisins
1 tablespoon cashew nuts
½ cup mixed dried fruit
2 cups ghee
4 cardamoms, powdered

Cook washed and drained rice and dal together in milk. When the rice is tender add the jaggery and cook till all is absorbed. Fry the raisins, nuts and other dried fruits in a few tablespoons of ghee. Add to the pongal with the rest of the ghee. Sprinkle with powdered cardamom seed.

Rice Flour Blancmange *(Phirni, Firni)*

2 pints (1135 ml) milk
2½ tablespoons rice flour
4 tablespoons sugar

12 white cardamoms, crushed
40 pistachio nuts or almonds,
    blanched

Mix the rice flour with enough milk to make a thin paste. Put the rest of the milk in a pan and bring to the boil. Cook on a medium heat for fifteen minutes, stirring continuously. Add sugar and keep cooking for another ten minutes. By now, the mixture should be fairly thick. Mix in the cardamom and nuts, leaving a few for sprinkling on top. Cook for a further five minutes. Pour into a bowl and decorate with the rest of the nuts. Serve chilled.

Creamed Semolina *(Khīr sūji)*

2 tablespoons ghee or butter
4 tablespoons semolina (suji)
1½ pints (850 ml) milk
5 tablespoons soft brown sugar

2 tablespoons sultanas
10 white cardamoms, skinned
    and crushed

Heat ghee and gently fry the semolina in a heavy pan for about five minutes, stirring continuously. When the ghee separates from the semolina, pour on the milk and stir in the sugar and sultanas. Keep stirring till the mixture thickens. Mix in the crushed cardamom and cook gently for 15-20 minutes. Serve hot or cold.

Creamed Vermicelli *(Khir savia)*

1 tablespoon ghee or butter
6 cloves
6 white cardamoms, skinned
    and crushed
1 cup broken vermicelli
3 cups milk

3 tablespoons sugar
1 tablespoon sultanas
1 tablespoon almonds,
    blanched and chopped
1 tablespoon pistachio nuts,
    chopped

Heat ghee and gently fry the cloves and half the cardamom for about two minutes. Add the vermicelli and fry till golden. Pour on the milk, bring to the boil and cook for ten minutes. Stir in the sugar, sultanas and nuts and continue cooking for a further fifteen minutes or until the desired consistency is obtained. Stir to prevent sticking. Pour into a dish and decorate with the rest of the cardamom. Serve hot or cold. Extra flavour and colour may be added by dissolving a pinch of saffron in a dessertspoon of rosewater and stirring into nearly cooked savia. Some cooks prefer this khir to be dry. Simply continue cooking the mixture gently till the excess moisture has been driven off. Serve with cream.

Muslims give khir savia (Sevian zarda) to their friends during the Id festival. It is a very nourishing dish, easily digested after a long fast.

Royal Bread (*Shāhi tukara*)

4–6 slices white bread
4 tablespoons ghee or butter
½ cup sugar
½ cup water
1 cup double cream

12 almonds, blanched and chopped
4 white cardamoms, skinned and crushed
1 tablespoon rosewater

Cut bread in cubes and fry in ghee till golden. Drain and put into a dish. Boil sugar and water to make a thick syrup. Pour over the fried bread and leave to soak for fifteen minutes. Pour cream over the cubes, garnish with the nuts and cardamom and sprinkle with rosewater. Serve chilled. Extra garnishes could include ground almonds mixed with the cream, chopped pistachio nuts and fried sultanas.

Condensed Milk Sweet (*Rabri*)

2 pints (1130 ml) full-cream milk
2 tablespoons sugar
1 teaspoon rosewater
1 tablespoon almonds, blanched and chopped

1 tablespoon pistachio nuts, chopped
6 white cardamoms, skinned and ground

Boil the milk, stirring continuously, till it is reduced to a quarter of

147

the quantity. The equivalent in condensed milk could be used. Stir in the sugar. Remove from heat, allow to cool and stir in the rosewater. Pour into a dish and garnish with the chopped nuts and cardamom. Serve chilled. This dish may be made more quickly by making the khoya from full-cream powdered milk but the taste will not be the same.

Flavoured Curd and Nut Sweet *(Shrīkand)*

The cowherd *(gopa)* of Mughal times took rice and curds along with vegetables and *Sikhram* which was made of curd, sugar, grated coconut and saffron. Shrikand is made all over India with local variations in ingredients. In Gujerat it is eaten with a bhajia and puris.

20 fl. oz (570 ml) yogurt
2 cups sugar
pinch of saffron
1 dessertspoon rosewater
10 white cardamoms,
   skinned and ground

1 tablespoon almonds,
   blanched and chopped
1 tablespoon pistachio nuts,
   chopped

Put the yogurt in a muslin bag and allow to hang overnight to extract the excess water. Dissolve the saffron in rosewater and beat into the curd. Mix in the rest of the ingredients and beat again. Serve chilled.

In Nepal, cloves, cinnamon and pepper are added with the cardamom to give a more spicy flavour.

Indian Ice Cream *(Kulfi)*

2 dessertspoons rice flour
2 pints (1130 ml) full-cream
   milk
4 oz (113 g) sugar
3 oz (85 g) khoya (see under
   Basic Ingredients)
4 white cardamoms, skinned
   and ground

1 dessertspoon almonds,
   blanched and chopped
1 dessertspoon pistachio nuts,
   chopped
2 teaspoons rosewater

Mix the rice flour with enough milk to make a thick paste. Boil the rest of the milk till it is reduced to half the quantity. Stir in the rice flour paste and sugar. Remove from the heat and add the rest of the ingredients. Mix well and put in the freezing tray of the refrigerator. Serve as ice cream.

Pistachio Ice Cream

4 fl. oz (113 ml) single cream
1 large can evaporated milk
4 oz (113 ml) sugar
2 tablespoons pistachio nuts, finely chopped

a few drops almond essence
a few drops green colouring
2 teaspoons gelatine
2 tablespoons hot water

Mix the cream and evaporated milk. Stir in the sugar till it dissolves. Add the nuts, almond essence and colouring. Dissolve the gelatine in hot water and stir into the ice cream. Allow to freeze. Whisk with a fork before it sets to prevent ice forming.

Banana Ice Cream

4 fl. oz (113 ml) single cream
1 large can evaporated milk
2 ripe bananas
lemon juice
5 oz (140 g) soft brown sugar

1 tablespoon cashew nuts, chopped
2 teaspoons gelatine
2 tablespoons hot water

Mix cream and evaporated milk. Mash the bananas, squeezing on a few drops of lemon juice. Add sugar and stir in till it dissolves. Add to this the milk mixture. Dissolve the gelatine in hot water and stir into the ice cream. Sprinkle with nuts. Allow to freeze. Whisk with a fork before it sets to prevent ice forming.

Any variations of these ice cream recipes may be used by substituting other fruit for the bananas, adding the appropriate flavouring and colouring as desired. Ginger ice cream can be made with 2 tablespoons of chopped fresh or preserved ginger or a few drops of ginger wine.

Semolina Pudding (*Sūji halva*)

4 tablespoons ghee
1 tablespoon sultanas
1 cup semolina (suji)
4 white cardamoms, skinned
   and ground
1 cup sugar
4 cloves

small piece cinnamon
3 cups water
1 tablespoon rosewater
1 tablespoon almonds,
   blanched and chopped
1 tablespoon pistachio nuts or
   cashew nuts, chopped

Heat ghee and fry the sultanas and semolina till the semolina is golden, stirring continuously. Add the cardamom, sugar, cloves, cinnamon and water. Mix well and gently cook for a further fifteen minutes. When all the excess water has been driven off, pour into a shallow dish. Sprinkle with rosewater and decorate with nuts. Serve hot or cold.

Coconut Dumplings (*Nariyal pitta*)

1 coconut
8 oz (225 g) sugar
2 tablespoons ghee or butter
1 teaspoon vanilla essence
   (optional)
6 white cardamoms,
   skinned and ground

1 tablespoon sultanas
1 tablespoon almonds,
   blanched and chopped
1 cup rice flour

Grate the coconut into a pan and mix with sugar, a tablespoon of ghee and 4 tablespoons water. Heat gently till the sugar dissolves and the mixture dries up. Remove from heat, cool and stir in the vanilla, cardamom, sultanas and almonds. Mix the rice flour and a tablespoon of ghee in a pan. Stir in a little water until a thick paste is formed. Continue stirring over a low heat till all the water has evaporated and the dough leaves the sides of the pan. Knead this dough and make into small balls with the help of a little ghee. Flatten the balls and place a teaspoonful of the coconut mixture on each. Bring the edges together, seal and roll up again. Put the dumplings in a greased steamer and steam till well cooked and firm. These dumplings may also be deep-fried in ghee or baked in a moderate oven, using puff-pastry instead of rice flour pastry. Serve hot or cold.

Stuffed Banana Balls (Kervai)

3–6 bananas
ghee or butter
1 tablespoon rice flour
1 tablespoon almonds,
  blanched and chopped
1 tablespoon pistachio nuts,
  chopped

1 tablespoon sultanas
2 tablespoons soft brown
  sugar
2 white cardamoms, skinned
  skinned and ground
1 dessertspoon poppy seeds

Peel the bananas and fry gently in a little ghee till tender. Remove and mash. Add the rice flour and mix well. Lightly fry the nuts and sultanas till golden. Stir in the sugar, cardamom and poppy seeds. Form the mashed banana into balls and stuff with the nut mixture. Roll up and deep-fry in ghee. Serve hot.

Pancakes (Mālpura)

2 cups plain flour (maida)
2 cups semolina (suji)
2 cups sugar
20 fl. oz (570 ml) yogurt
6 green cardamoms, skinned
  and ground

pinch of saffron
ghee
1 teaspoon aniseed or fennel
  and some whole peppercorns
  may be added to give a more
  piquant flavour.

Mix all the ingredients to make a thick batter, adding water if necessary. Cover and leave overnight. Next day add another ½ cup of semolina and mix well. Fry in ghee like pancakes, dropping in tablespoons of the batter at a time. Cook on both sides. The edges should be crisp with a soft centre. Serve hot. Malpuras, like dosas, are a favourite for breakfast in the rainy season. They are served with rice pudding in some areas.

Pickles and Chutneys

Pickles

Lemon

10 lemons
2 tablespoons salt
1 dessertspoon turmeric

1 dessertspoon garam masala
1 teaspoon chilli powder
(optional)

Cut five of the lemons in small pieces. Sprinkle with salt and the spices and put in a jar. Pour on the juice from the other five lemons. Cover tightly and keep in a warm place for a week, shaking the jar every day. The pickle is ready when the skins are tender.

Sweet Cauliflower

1 large cauliflower
4 oz (113 g) ginger, sliced
2 tablespoons salt
1 dessertspoon turmeric powder
1 teaspoon chilli powder

1 tablespoon mustard seeds
1 dessertspoon garam masala
4 tablespoons soft brown sugar
3 tablespoons vinegar
juice of 1 lemon

Break the cauliflower in small pieces, wash and put in a little water. Bring to the boil, drain and cool. Mix in a bowl with the ginger.

Sprinkle on the salt, turmeric, chilli, mustard seeds and garam masala. Mix well. Dissolve the sugar in vinegar and lemon juice and boil together for a few minutes. Pour over the cauliflower. Mix again and put in jars. Keep in a warm place for a few days.

Carrots, parsnips, turnips and cabbage can be pickled in the same way.

Carrot

2 lbs (900 g) carrots
salt
vinegar
3 tablespoons mustard seeds

12 green chillies
4 oz (113 g) ginger, sliced
4 cloves garlic, chopped

Cut the carrots in long slices and cut each slice in half. Put in a dish and sprinkle with salt. Leave in a warm place for three days. Wash in vinegar and put in a mixing bowl. Add the mustard seeds, whole chillies, ginger and garlic and mix well. Put in jars and cover the pickle with vinegar. Screw up and shake well. Leave in a warm place for a few days.

Mixed Vegetable

4 lbs (1·8 kg) turnips or radishes
2 lbs (900 g) cauliflower
2 lbs (900 g) young carrots
1 lb (450 g) peas

4 cloves garlic
4 oz (113 g) ginger, chopped
4 oz (113 g) onions, chopped
1 pint (570 ml) sesame seed oil

1 tablespoon chilli powder
1 tablespoon garam masala
1 tablespoon mustard seeds
2 teaspoons turmeric powder

3–4 tablespoons salt
3 cups vinegar
2 lbs (900 g) soft brown sugar

Peel, wash and trim the vegetables. Slice the turnips and carrots and cut the cauliflower in small pieces. Put in a pan of water and boil till they become tender. Remove and drain. Meanwhile, grind the garlic, ginger and onions to a paste. Heat oil and fry the paste. Add the rest of the spices and salt and fry for a few minutes. Cool and mix with the vegetables. Put in jars and keep in a warm place for three days, giving the jars a good shake every day. Boil sugar and vinegar for a few minutes. Cool and pour over the pickle. Keep in a warm place for a further two days. Screw up tight.

Aubergine

3 lbs (1·35 kg) aubergines
1 tablespoon dry red chillies or
    chilli powder
1 tablespoon turmeric powder
2 oz (57 g) ginger
10 cloves garlic
½ pint (284 ml) sesame seed oil

a few curry leaves
2 teaspoons fenugreek seeds
2 teaspoons cumin seeds
2 teaspoons mustard seeds
8 green chillies
vinegar
2 tablespoons salt

Trim and wash the aubergines. Quarter and slice into small pieces. Grind the red chillies, turmeric, ginger and garlic to a paste. Heat oil and fry the paste with the curry leaves, fenugreek, cumin and mustard seeds. Mix in the aubergines and green chillies. Pour over enough vinegar to cover. Add salt and simmer till the aubergines are tender. Cool, bottle and make airtight.

My wife's grandmother would have added 1½ cups of sugar and double the amount of garlic to the recipe. This modifies the taste. Experiment to see which type of pickle you prefer.

Lemon Achar

1 tablespoon mustard seeds
1 tablespoon black peppercorns

1 tablespoon fennel seeds
1 teaspoon cumin seeds

½ teaspoon chilli powder
1 teaspoon salt

8 lemons
1 pint (570 ml) mustard oil

Mix all the spices and salt. Cut the lemons in quarters and remove the pips. Sprinkle with the spices and put in jars. Boil the oil and pour the hot oil over the lemons. Make airtight.

Vegetable Achar

1 small cauliflower
6 onions, peeled and sliced
6 gherkins or courgettes, sliced
6 green chillies
2 tablespoons mustard seeds

1 tablespoon fennel seeds
1 teaspoon chilli powder
1 tablespoon salt
1 pint (570 ml) mustard oil

Cut the cauliflower in small pieces and mix well with the rest of the vegetables, spices and salt. Put in jars. Boil the oil, cool and pour over the pickle. Cover and keep in a warm place for a week. Make airtight.

Chutneys

Chutneys which can be kept have to be cooked and bottled.

Mixed Fruit

8 oz (225 g) cooking apples
8 oz (225 g) pears
6 oz (170 g) dried apricots
2 tablespoons sultanas
12 oz (340 g) soft brown sugar
½ pint (284 ml) vinegar
1 teaspoon garam masala

12 cloves garlic, sliced
1 tablespoon finely chopped
  ginger
1 dessertspoon salt
1 teaspoon caraway seeds or
  cumin seeds

Peel and core the apples and pears. Cut all the fruit in small pieces and mix in the rest of the ingredients in a pan. Boil gently for 40 minutes. Cool and bottle.

Carrot

2 lbs (900 g) carrots
1 tablespoon salt
4 cloves garlic, sliced
2 tablespoons mustard seeds
2 teaspoons cumin seeds

2 teaspoons finely chopped
  ginger
1 tablespoon black peppercorns
1 cup soft brown sugar
½ pint (284 ml) vinegar

Wash, scrape and trim the carrots. Cut in small pieces and mix with the rest of the ingredients in a pan. Boil gently till the carrots are tender. Cool and bottle.

Tomato

1 lb (450 g) cooking apples
2 lbs (900 g) fresh or tinned
  tomatoes
2 oz (57 g) ginger

1 oz (28 g) garlic
1 teaspoon salt
1 teaspoon chilli powder
½ pint (284 ml) vinegar

Peel and core the apples. Cut the apples and tomatoes in small pieces. Pound the ginger and garlic together. Mix with the apples and tomatoes in a pan. Sprinkle with salt and chilli powder and cover with vinegar. Cook until a thick pulp forms. Cool and bottle.

This recipe can be supplemented by adding the following ingredients to 2 lbs (900 g) tomatoes:

1 small onion, finely chopped
1 dessertspoon raisins or
  sultanas
1 tablespoon finely chopped ginger
2 cloves garlic, finely chopped
8 cardamoms, skinned and ground

6 cloves
1 teaspoon chilli powder
2 bay leaves
1½ teaspoons salt
1 cup soft brown sugar
½ pint (284 ml) vinegar

Mix the ingredients and cook as above. Bottle when cool.

Ginger and Garlic

1 lb (450 g) ginger
12 oz (340 g) garlic
2 tablespoons mustard seeds
2 teaspoons chilli powder

2 teaspoons salt
1 cup soft brown sugar
½ pint (284 ml) vinegar

Pound the ginger and garlic. Mix with the other ingredients and cook gently till the right consistency is formed. Bottle when cool.

Pineapple

1½ lbs (680 g) pineapple
1 tablespoon salt
8 cloves garlic
2 tablespoons ginger, chopped

8 oz (225 g) raisins
1 cup soft brown sugar
½ pint (284 ml) vinegar

Peel and trim the pineapple and cut in small pieces. Put in a pan and sprinkle with salt. Pound the garlic and ginger and add to the pineapple. Mix in the rest of the ingredients and boil gently to form a chutney. Bottle when cool.

Rhubarb

1½ lbs (680 g) rhubarb
2 teaspoons ginger, chopped
4 cloves garlic
1 teaspoon chilli powder

2 tablespoons mustard seeds
2 tablespoons ground almonds
8 oz (225 g) soft brown sugar
1 pint (570 ml) vinegar

Wash and trim the rhubarb. Cut in small pieces. Pound the ginger and garlic. Mix all the ingredients and cook gently to form a chutney. Bottle when cool.

Sweet

2 lbs (900 g) cooking apples
1 tablespoon ginger, chopped
1 tablespoon garlic, chopped
1 lb (450 g) raisins

1 tablespoon dried red chillies
1 teaspoon salt
1 lb (450 g) soft brown sugar
½ pint (284 ml) vinegar

Peel and core the apples and cut in pieces. Pound the ginger and garlic. Mix all the ingredients together and cook gently to form a chutney. Bottle when cool.

Fresh Chutneys

Fresh chutneys need to be consumed as soon as possible and will not keep well unless refrigerated. The fresh taste and aroma of the chutney are selected to go with particular dishes. Experiment to find the ones you like best. Several chutneys are usually served with a curry. In India they are made during the preparation of masalas and vary according to the season. Most fresh chutneys are improved by being served slightly chilled.

Coconut

4 tablespoons grated coconut
1 tablespoon chopped ginger
1–2 green chillies, finely chopped and seeded

1 tablespoon finely chopped coriander leaves
lemon juice

Pound the coconut and ginger. Add the chilli and coriander leaf. Sprinkle with lemon juice to make a paste. Most coconut chutneys originate from South India. The following chutney goes well with idlis (see recipe):

½ coconut, grated
4–6 green chillies
1 tablespoon split yellow peas (channa dal)
1 teaspoon salt
1 cup yogurt

1 tablespoon ghee
½ teaspoon mustard seeds
½ teaspoon split black peas (urhad dal)
a few curry leaves

Grind the grated coconut, chillies, gram dal and salt to a paste. Beat the yogurt and stir in the paste. Heat ghee and lightly fry the mustard seeds, urhad dal and curry leaves till the mustard seeds sputter. Stir into the chutney.

Potato

4 potatoes
2–4 green chillies, finely chopped

½ teaspoon salt
¼ teaspoon black pepper
juice of 1 lemon

Cook the potatoes till tender. Peel and chop in small pieces. Mix with the chillies. Sprinkle with salt, pepper and lemon juice. A cup of beaten curd and a teaspoon of cumin seeds or powder will vary the taste and consistency of the chutney.

Cucumber

1 lb (450 g) cucumber
1 lb (450 g) onion, finely
  chopped
1 teaspoon salt

½ teaspoon pepper or chilli
  powder
juice of 1 lemon

Peel and chop the cucumber. Mix with an equal quantity of onion. Sprinkle with salt, pepper and lemon juice. Add 2 cloves garlic and a tablespoon finely chopped coriander leaves for extra flavour.

Mint

½ cup mint leaves
2 green chillies, seeded and
  finely chopped
1 teaspoon chopper ginger

2 tablespoons chopped onion
1 clove garlic
1 teaspoon sugar
juice of 1 lemon

Wash the mint leaves and grind to a paste with the rest of the ingredients, adding the lemon juice at the end.

Mint and Coriander

1 tablespoon tamarind pulp
1 tablespoon coriander leaves
1 tablespoon mint leaves

1 green chilli
1 teaspoon sugar
1 teaspoon salt

Soak the tamarind in half a cup of hot water to extract the juice. Wash the green leaves and grind together with the chilli. Sprinkle with sugar and salt and the tamarind juice or juice of half a lemon.

Carrot

8 oz (225 g) young carrots
1 small onion, chopped
1 tablespoon chopped ginger

2 tablespoons coriander leaf,
  finely chopped
1 teaspoon salt
juice of ½ lemon

Wash and trim the carrots. Chop and pound with the onion and ginger. Mix with the coriander leaf. Sprinkle with salt and lemon juice.

Sweet

4 tablespoons tamarind pulp
4 tablespoons soft brown sugar
  or jaggery
1 teaspoon chilli powder
1 teaspoon coriander seeds

1 teaspoon fennel seeds
1 teaspoon cumin seeds
½ teaspoon salt
1 tablespoon chopped
  coriander leaf

Soak the tamarind in a cup of hot water. Grind the sugar with the other ingredients. Sprinkle with the strained tamarind juice, or juice of half a lemon, and coriander leaf.

Coriander

½ cup coriander leaves
1 tablespoon grated coconut
2 cloves garlic
1 teaspoon chopped ginger

2 tablespoons onion, chopped
2–4 green chillies
½ teaspoon salt
juice of ½ lemon

Grind together the coriander leaves, coconut, garlic, ginger, onion and chillies. Sprinkle with salt and lemon juice.

Onion

2 onions, chopped
a few mint leaves
1 teaspoon chilli powder

1 teaspoon cumin seeds
1 teaspoon salt
juice of 1 lemon

Grind together the onion and mint. Sprinkle with the rest of the ingredients and mix well.

Beetroot

1 cup chopped cooked beetroot
½ cup dried or stoned fresh
   dates, chopped
2 tablespoons chopped onion
a few mint leaves

2 tablespoons grated coconut
½ teaspoon chilli powder
pinch of black pepper
juice of 1 lemon or equivalent
   in vinegar

Mix the ingredients and sprinkle with chilli powder, pepper, lemon juice or vinegar. This recipe can be used with bananas by substituting the same amount for the beetroot.

Tomato

1 lb (450 g) tomatoes, finely
   chopped
1 small onion, finely chopped
1 teaspoon salt

1 teaspoon chilli powder
1 teaspoon garam masala
juice of 1 lemon or vinegar

Mix the tomatoes and onions and sprinkle with the rest of the ingredients. Mix well. Half a cup of chopped dates may be added to make the chutney sweeter.

Aubergine

1 large aubergine
2 green chillies, seeded and
   finely chopped
1 onion, finely chopped

½ cup grated coconut
1 teaspoon salt
juice of 1 lemon

Roast or grill the aubergine till the skin is burnt and the flesh is tender. Peel and mash. Mix with the rest of the ingredients.

Date

8 oz (225 g) dried or fresh
 stoned dates
1 teaspoon turmeric powder
1 tablespoon chopped
 coriander leaves

1 teaspoon salt
2 green chillies, finely chopped
juice of 1 lemon

Pound the ingredients together to form a chutney, adding a little water if necessary.

Curd

This is a South Indian chutney usually served with dosas:

1 tablespoon ghee
2 teaspoons split black peas
 (urhad dal)
2 teaspoons split yellow peas
 (channa dal)
1 teaspoon mustard seeds
$\frac{1}{2}$ teaspoon cumin seeds
2 tablespoons grated coconut

6 green chillies, chopped
1 dessertspoon chopped ginger
a few curry leaves
1 cup yogurt
juice of $\frac{1}{2}$ lemon
1 teaspoon salt
$\frac{1}{2}$ teaspoon sambhar masala

Heat ghee and fry the urhad dal and channa dal for a few minutes. Remove and fry the mustard seeds and cumin seeds till the mustard seeds sputter. Grind the coconut, chillies, ginger, curry leaves and fried dal with a little water to make a paste. Add the fried mustard seeds and cumin. Stir the mixture into beaten yogurt and sprinkle with lemon juice, salt and sambhar masala. Mix well.

The Tale of the Squash Maker

' "I see what you mean," laughed the merchant. And there he
had to take his leave.' 'Quite a character, your merchant,' said
the cook, opening his eyes and reaching for another smoke. Then
his eyes narrowed. 'But wandering monks are strange men, you
know. There's a village near here where quite an ordinary incident
occurred the other day, but it made me think afterwards. Your
merchant friend's remarks reminded me of it. A squashmaker
had climbed a tree in search of its fruit. As he climbed higher, he
noticed the fruit becoming choicer in quality. He tasted some and
indeed the higher he climbed the more delicious it tasted. The
best must be at the top then, he surmised. He reached the very
top of the tree and had filled his basket when he found that he
could not climb down again. Panicking, he hung his basket from
a branch, cupped both hands and shouted for help. Soon villagers
came running, but, seeing his predicament, none could offer help.
The poor man screamed all the louder. The headman was called
but there was no way of reaching the fellow short of climbing
the tree and getting in the same fix. "Don't worry!" he shouted
encouragingly, "we'll think of something in a minute." Just then
he noticed a wandering monk passing by. "Oh, sir, help us!" he
cried. "See the trouble our friend is in. Please say a prayer for him.
Ask God to get him down!" "All right," said the monk. "I'll help
him." And with that he bent and picked up a stone and threw it
at the man, who was still shouting hoarsely from the top of
the tree. He cried out in pain as the stone struck his thigh. The
headman looked aghast but was too dumbfounded to speak. Again
the monk bent down and, finding a larger stone, threw it with
even greater force. With a shriek the stranded man sought cover
and, reaching for a lower branch, quickly swung out of sight.
In minutes he had reached the ground and rushed towards the
headman. "Where's that cowardly scoundrel!" he shouted,
waving his fist. The headman turned, but the monk was nowhere
to be found. . . .'

Drinks and Soups

Curd drink (*Lassi*)

To make 1 glass:
Beat half a glass of yogurt with half a glass of cold water, add sugar to taste. These proportions may be varied to suit individual taste. In summer serve chilled.

Falūda

Faluda is India's exotic version of the milk shake. Kulfi (see recipe) should be mixed with milk and faluda (*sabja*) seeds. Here is a recipe which makes this nourishing and refreshing drink more easily available:

4 tablespoons condensed milk	2 tablespoons cooked tapioca
8 tablespoons milk	2 teaspoons rosewater
1 tablespoon sugar	

Combine the ingredients and add cold water if necessary to make enough for four glasses. Top with ice cream, kulfi or cream. Serve chilled. In India, faluda is often sold as a gaily coloured drink. Add colouring or fruit extract.

Honey Milk

1 cup milk
2 teaspoons honey

pinch of cardamom powder
or nutmeg

Heat the milk but do not allow to boil. Stir in the honey and serve sprinkled with cardamom. This may be drunk hot as a nourishing daytime drink or nightcap or chill to make a refresher. A quick nourishing drink, useful as an energiser, may be prepared by stirring liquid honey into a glass of milk. Top with crushed nuts and stir well.

Mango Squash

Squashes are fresh fruit juices preserved in syrup.

15 fl. oz (426 ml) water
20 oz (570 g) sugar
2 teaspoons citric acid

1 lb (450 g) mango pulp
yellow or orange colouring

Mix water, sugar and citric acid and boil till the sugar is dissolved and the syrup thickens. Cool. If tinned mangoes are used, pound them finely or put in a liquidiser and add to the syrup. Pour in the tinned syrup. Stir in the colouring. Pour into sterilised bottles and store in a cool place.

Orange Squash

1 pint (570 ml) fresh orange
  juice
14 oz (400 g) sugar

$1\frac{1}{2}$ teaspoons citric acid
orange colouring

Mix the orange juice, sugar and citric acid and stir till the sugar is dissolved and the mixture thickens. Add the colouring and pour into sterilised bottles.

Lichi Squash

2 lbs (900 g) lichis (Chinese
   gooseberries)
2 cups water

1½ lbs (680 g) sugar
1 dessertspoon citric acid

Pound the lichis and strain off the juice. If tinned lichis are used, add the syrup to make up to 15 fl. oz (426 ml) juice. Add water, sugar and citric acid. Warm till the sugar is dissolved and the mixture thickens. Cool and pour into sterilised bottles.

Pineapple Squash

15 fl. oz (426 ml) pineapple juice
½ pint (284 ml) water
½ lb (284 g) sugar

1 teaspoon citric acid
1 teaspoon pineapple essence

Mix the ingredients and warm until the sugar dissolves and the mixture thickens. Cool and pour into sterilised bottles.

Almond Sherbert (*Sharbat badām*)

4 tablespoons almonds
1½ lbs (680 g) sugar
8 white cardamoms, skinned
   and ground

1 tablespoon rosewater
a few drops almond essence

Blanch the almonds in hot water and leave to cool. Peel and grind to a smooth paste. Make up to 15 fl. oz (426 ml) with water. Strain and add sugar. Heat till the sugar dissolves and the mixture thickens, removing any scum. Add cardamom, cool and add rosewater and almond essence. Store in sterilised bottles.

Almond Drink

4 tablespoons almonds
4 tablespoons sugar

2 tablespoons orange juice
2 pints (1136 ml) water

Blanch the almonds in hot water and leave to cool. Peel and grind with sugar, orange juice and a little water to a smooth paste. Put in a bowl and add the rest of the water. Leave for two hours. Serve diluted with cold water.

Sandalwood Sherbert *(Sharbat sandal)*

1 tablespoon sandalwood
  powder
15 fl. oz (426 ml) water

1½ lbs (680 g) sugar
1 tablespoon rosewater

Soak the sandalwood powder overnight in the water. Simmer in a closed pan for about an hour to extract the flavour. Strain and make up to the original quantity with water. Add sugar and heat till the sugar dissolves and the mixture thickens. Cool, stir in the rosewater and store in sterilised bottles.

Rose Sherbert *(Sharbat gulāb)*

1 heaped tablespoon dried rose
  petals

1½ lbs (680 g) sugar
2 tablespoons rosewater

Soak petals overnight in ½ pint (284 ml) water. Strain. Mix sugar and 15 fl. oz (426 ml) water. Add the rose petal extract and boil the syrup till it thickens. Remove any scum. Cool and stir in the rosewater. Store in sterilised bottles.

Lemon Water *(Nimbū pāni)*

juice of 3 lemons
1½ tablespoons sugar

3 teaspoons rosewater

Mix the strained lemon juice with sugar and stir till it dissolves. Add 4 glasses of water and the rosewater. Serve chilled.

Lemon Syrup

1 teaspoon lemon essence
5 tablespoons citric acid

3½ lbs (1575 g) sugar
2 pints (1136 ml) water

Mix the ingredients and boil to make a thick syrup. Cool and bottle. Serve a tablespoonful to a glass of water.

Lemonade Syrup

3 lbs (1350 g) sugar
3 pints (1700 ml) water
1 tablespoon tartaric acid
  powder

1 dessertspoon lemon essence

Boil the sugar and water for five minutes. Stir in the acid. Cool and add the lemon essence. Bottle.

Kashmiri Tea

Two kinds of Kashmiri tea are drunk during or after meals. Salty tea is a dark red-brown and taken with cream. Here is a recipe for sweet tea (*kahva*). As the tea used in Kashmir is unobtainable here, a good substitute is a mixture of green tea and Darjeeling or Orange Pekoe in the proportion 3:1.

2½ cups milk + 2½ cups water
  or 5 cups water
3 level teaspoons green tea
1 teaspoon Darjeeling or
  Orange Pekoe Tea
6 green cardamoms

6 almonds, blanched and
  chopped
1 teaspoon pine nuts, shelled
small piece cinnamon
2 cloves

Stew gently for 15–30 minutes. Strain and serve hot, adding sugar to taste. Sweet tea is sometimes additionally perfumed with saffron. Kashmiris make their tea in a samovar and, like Tibetans and the people of the frontier countries, enjoy tea-drinking at any time of day.

Aniseed Tea

4 tablespoons aniseed   4 cups black tea

Boil the aniseed in two cups of water till tender and the water is
aromatised. Strain into the black tea. Add milk and sugar to taste
and pour into glasses. Crushed ice may be added to chill.

Cumin Appetiser *(Jīra pāni)*

An appetiser from ancient times which has digestive properties and
is often served with meals on festive occasions. It may be served
with gol gappas (see recipe).

4 tablespoons tamarind pulp
1 teaspoon dried mint or a
   few fresh leaves
2 tablespoons cumin powder
3 teaspoons salt

1 tablespoon ginger, chopped
1 teaspoon paprika
½ teaspoon garam masala
1 tablespoon sugar
4 tablespoons lemon juice

Soak the tamarind in a pint (570 ml) of water overnight. Pound and
strain off the juice. Add a further pint of water. Grind the rest of the
ingredients and add to the tamarind water. Add lemon juice and ice
to chill. Stir well before serving.

Pepperwater *(Rasam)*

Pepperwater is another digestive, often served after the meal.

1 tablespoon tamarind pulp
1 teaspoon black peppercorns
1 teaspoon cumin seeds
4 cloves garlic
1 pint (570 ml) water
1 dessertspoon coriander leaves,
   finely chopped

1 teaspoon salt
1 tablespoon ghee
1 teaspoon mustard seeds
½ onion, finely chopped

Soak the tamarind in half a cup of hot water and extract the juice.
Grind the peppercorns, cumin and garlic and mix with the tamarind

juice. Add water, coriander leaves and salt. Heat ghee in a pan and fry the mustard seeds and onion till the onion turns golden. Add the pepperwater mixture and simmer for a few minutes. Serve hot.

Mulligatawny Soup

This South Indian soup was originally used as a cure for indigestion and was known as 'pepperwater' in Tamil. Like the previous recipe, it was made from peppercorns boiled in water with tamarind. In the course of time, stock and other ingredients have come to be added and garam masala is frequently used instead of pepper.

1 cup red lentils (masur dal)
2 onions, finely sliced
bay leaf
2 tablespoons ghee
1 clove garlic, finely chopped

1 tablespoon garam masala
2 pints vegetable stock
1 teaspoon salt
½ cup coconut milk (optional)

Wash the lentils and leave to soak for a few hours. Drain and boil in a pint (570 ml) of water with a sliced onion and some bay leaves till soft. Heat ghee and fry the garlic and rest of the onion till golden. Add the garam masala and fry for a few minutes. Add to the dal with stock and salt. Bring to the boil and add coconut milk. Serve hot with lemon and a little boiled rice.

Lemon Rasam

1 cup split black peas
  (urhad dal)
1 teaspoon cumin powder
½ teaspoon black pepper
1 teaspoon salt
juice of 2 lemons
1 tablespoon ghee

1 teaspoon mustard seeds
1 teaspoon finely chopped
  ginger
1 teaspoon finely chopped
  green chilli
coriander leaves, chopped

Wash the dal and boil in water till soft. Add enough water to make it up to a thin soup. Stir in cumin, pepper, salt and lemon juice. Heat ghee in a pan and fry the mustard seeds, ginger and chilli till the mustard seeds begin to sputter. Stir into the dal soup. Serve hot sprinkled with coriander leaves.

Tomato Rasam

4 large tomatoes
3 pints (1700 ml) water
2 teaspoons salt
1 teaspoon cumin powder
¼ teaspoon black pepper
1 tablespoon ghee

6 cloves garlic, finely chopped
1 onion, finely sliced
1 teaspoon mustard seeds
½ teaspoon chilli powder
coriander leaves, chopped

Chop the tomatoes and boil in water with salt till soft. Mash and stir in the cumin and pepper. Heat ghee and fry the garlic and onion till golden. Add the mustard seeds and chilli powder and fry for a further two minutes. Stir into the tomato soup. Serve hot sprinkled with coriander leaves.

Like many after-meal digestives, this recipe comes from South India.

Note on Pronunciation of Indian Words

Indian languages are written phonetically and all the letters are pronounced. Except for 'ch' and 'sh', an 'h' after a consonant should be pronounced separately. 'E' and 'o' are long vowels; 'i' is pronounced long at the end of a word.

Pronounce 'a' as 'u' in the English word 'but'
'ā' as 'a' in the English word 'father'
'i' as 'i' in the English word 'bit'
'ī' as 'ee' in the English word 'meet'
'u' as 'oo' in the English word 'book'
'ū' as 'oo' in the English word 'moon'

The Tale of the Pandit

'Ah!' sighed the cook's friend. 'There are such men. What secret wisdom do they possess, or are they just fools and it is we who are too sophisticated to see it?' 'Careful now, are you deliberately confusing the wisdom of wise men with the wisdom of fools, or are you trying to lead into another story? I don't envy the fool his wisdom at least. A knowledgeable man like yourself, he might be admired.' The cook waved his arm and his voice rose to emphasise the point. 'If I envy anyone, it's you, my old friend. How I wish I had your knowledge. We spend so much of our lives eating, yet how many of us take the trouble to study the art of cooking?' Before the cook could reply, the two friends were startled by the flustered entry of the owner of the house. 'Deviprasad!' he cried. 'Do me the favour of furnishing me with some fortifying preparation of yours. I feel terrible! The bottom is falling out of my world!' 'But, sir, what causes this upset in your person?' the cook inquired. By now, both men had jumped to their feet. 'Sit down here, sir,' the cook's friend motioned. 'I don't know whether I have just been insulted or otherwise!' The pandit sagged in his chair, his face twisted with painful memory. 'I answered the knock of a monk who had had the temerity to come to the main door. "What do you want?" I asked him, knowing full well that he was begging for food.' The cook and his friend nodded their understanding. ' "What do you have to offer?" the fellow retorted. Naturally, I was a little taken aback. "Do you know who I am?" I asked him angrily. "Why," he smiled, "do you know who you are?" It was the way he smiled at me, I suddenly felt completely at a loss. When I had recovered my composure, the fellow seemed to have vanished.' 'Amazing behaviour!' said the cook's friend, shaking his head. 'Oh, Deviprasad!' wailed the pandit, 'with all my years of study, with all my learning, in spite of my great reputation, I had no ready answer!' The cook looked at the pandit, then at his friend. The smokes had gone out. The room was quiet. His friend looked back at him.

Glossary

achar	a type of pickle
ālū	potato
andā	egg
arbi	yam
arū	peach
badām	almond
baingan	aubergine, eggplant
bandgobi	cabbage
barfi	milk sweet
batāta	potato
bāth	a rice dish (S. India)
besan	gram flour
Bhagavad Gītā	'The Song of the Lord', part of the Mahābharata that contains the teachings of Lord Krishna, an incarnation of the god Vishnu.
bharta	puréed vegetable
bhindi	Lady Finger, okra
bhujia	fried greens
channa	yellow peas
chapāti	flat bread made from wholewheat flour and water
chāval	rice
chenna	soft cheese made from curd (cottage cheese)
chukunda	beetroot
dahi	curd, yogurt
dāl	split peas
dam	technique of steaming
dhania	coriander
dosa	spicy pancake (S. India)
fūgath	vegetables fried with onions and masala
gājar	carrot
ghi	clarified butter, used since ancient times
gobi	cabbage
gūda	marrow
gulāb	rose, rosewater
haldi	turmeric
halva	heavy sweet made by reducing fruit or vegetable with sugar

idli	dumpling
jāman	milk ball
jīra	cumin
kabli channa	Bengal peas
kadū	pumpkin, marrow
Kashmīri	cooking style of Kashmir, one of the most northern parts of the Indian subcontinent
kela	banana, plantain
khichhari	rice and lentils cooked together
khir	a technique of creaming by cooking in milk
khira	cucumber
khoya	thick milk made by slowly driving off the water
khumbi	mushroom
kishmish	sultana
kofta	vegetable ball
korma	food cooked in curd
Mahābharata	great epic poem of India, said to have been written thousands of years ago by the god Ganapati to the dictation of the sage Vyasa, which has profoundly affected Indian life.
masāla	a mixture of spices used for flavouring and aromatising food.
masūr	red lentils
matar	peas
mīthe	sweet
moli	currying technique from Goa
Mughal	The Mughals brought to India an Islamic culture from central Asia. The Mughal shahs reigned from 1556–1784
mūli	radish
mūng	green pea
nān	flat bread baked in N. India
nimbū	lime, lemon
pachadi	vegetables and curd (S. India)
pandit	a Hindu scholar, originally a title signifying a degree of knowledge of the Sanskrit texts.
pāni	water (N. India), also *jal* (Hindi)
panir	hard cheese made from curd
parātha	flat bread made from wholewheat flour and fried in ghee
phali	vegetables, green beans, peanuts

phūlgobi	cauliflower
pīāz	onion
pistā	pistachio nut
pongal	S. Indian sweet rice (Tamil)
pulau	rice first fried in ghee, then cooked in a stock which should be fully absorbed.
pūri	small puffed breads fried in ghee
raita	vegetable in curd (N. India)
rajas	in Indian philosophy, the quality of action (Sanskrit)
rasgulla	curd ball
roti	bread
sabzi	vegetable
sādhu	a holy man
sāg	spinach, greens
sambhar	hot lentils, hot masala (S. India)
sattva	in Indian philosophy, the quality of harmony (Sanskrit)
savia	vermicelli
sev	vermicelli made from gram flour batter
shalgam	turnip
sharbat	drink prepared from flowers, bark, resins, etc.
simla mirch	green pepper, capsicum
sūji	semolina
tamas	in Indian philosophy, the quality of inertia (Sanskrit)
tamātar	tomato
tandūri	a form of baking using a clay oven (*tandūr*). N. India
tarkari	technique where vegetables are cooked in their own juice with ghee and the heat is raised at the end to impregnate taste and aroma
tikki	cutlet
til	sesame
urhad	black pea
vindālū	sour curry made in Goa